☙

The Little Book of
the Blessed Virgin Mary

Other books by Raoul Plus
from Sophia Institute Press:

Holy Simplicity

How to Pray Always

How to Pray Well

Progress in Divine Union

Raoul Plus, S.J.

The Little Book of
the Blessed Virgin Mary

Model of Christians, Cause of Our Joy

SOPHIA INSTITUTE PRESS
Manchester, New Hampshire

The Little Book of the Blessed Virgin Mary was formerly published in 1940 by Frederick Pustet Co., Inc., New York, under the title *Mary in Our Soul-Life*, using the translation by Sister Mary Bertille and Sister Mary St. Thomas from the original French. This 2010 edition by Sophia Institute Press includes minor editorial revisions.

On the cover: *Virgin and Child* (oil on panel) by Gerard David (c.1460-1523) Prado, Madrid, Spain / The Bridgeman Art Library.

Sophia Institute Press®
Box 5284, Manchester, NH 03108
1-800-888-9344
www.SophiaInstitute.com
Sophia Institute Press® is a registered trademark of Sophia Institute.

Nihil obstat: Arthur J. Scanlan, S.T., *Censor Librorum*
Imprimatur: +Francis J. Spellman, D.D. Archbishop of New York
New York, September 18, 1940

Library of Congress Cataloging-in-Publication Data

Plus, Raoul, 1882-1958.
    [Marie dans notre histoire divine. English]
    The little book of the Blessed Virgin Mary : model of Christians, cause
       of our joy / Raoul Plus.
       p. cm.
    Translated by Mary Bertille and Mary St. Thomas.
    Originally published: Mary in our soul-life. New York : F. Pustet Co.,
       1940. With minor editorial revisions.
    Includes bibliographical references.
    ISBN 978-1-933184-69-2 (pbk. : alk. paper) 1. Mary, Blessed Virgin,
       Saint — Theology. I. Title.

BT603.P58 2010
232.91 — dc22

                              2009049792

Contents

Book III
Mary's motherly heart

⚜

Foreword

If the number of books treating of methods to acquire sanctity were indicative of the holiness of a generation, then, indeed, could ours claim the halo of blessedness. But such is not the case. The ever-increasing production of ascetical literature evidences rather our yearning for a fuller participation in the life of God and our great need to be shown the way to attain it. For although every soul feels within it the persistent urging of Christ's injunction: *Be ye therefore perfect as your heavenly Father is perfect,*[1] nevertheless, modern materialism has so pitted its strength against spiritual endeavor that we often feel outwitted before we advance very far toward sainthood. Therefore, we eagerly thumb manuals of saintly living for successful techniques in the direction of our soul-life.

Too often, in the eagerness of our desire, we forget that, in pursuing the science of the saints, as in pursuing other sciences, original sources are to be studied first. We realize that progress in holiness is measured by growth in likeness to Christ, that perfect soul-life means Christ-life; yet we forget to go for guidance to her

[1] Cf. Matt. 5:48.

who beheld Christ daily *advance in wisdom and age and grace with God and men.*[2] We forget that Mary *kept all these words in her heart,*[3] thus giving us the most valuable manual of Christian perfection that can be had — her own heart. Christ invited us to read her heart so that our soul-life might not be *orphaned. Behold your Mother.*[4] Although Mary kept the *secrets of the King,* her heart is not a *closed book.* It is open wide for all to read. But we must read it as it is revealed in the events of her life, for Mary's attitudes, actions, words, and even her very silence, exemplifying as they did the principles treasured in her heart, teach us how to meet the advances of God so that our soul-life, like hers, may be *full of grace.*

Christ wants Mary *to mother* our soul-life as she mothered Him. The Holy Spirit cherishes her still as His Immaculate Spouse and desires to produce through her countless saints. Louis de Montfort insists that "One of the great reasons why the Holy Ghost does not now do startling wonders in our souls is because He does not find there a sufficiently great union with His faithful and inseparable Spouse."[5]

This book, then, makes an effort to weld our souls more closely to the Immaculate Spouse of the Holy Spirit. It is not a story of Mary's life, although it deals with some of the incidents of her life. It is an attempt, rather, to teach us to read her heart and to realize more profoundly the position *true theology* accords her in our soul-life.

Assumption of Our Lady, 1940

---

[2] Luke 2:52.

[3] Luke 2:51.

[4] Cf. John 19:27.

[5] St. Louis de Montfort (1673-1716; secular priest who founded the Sisters of the Divine Wisdom and the Missionary Priests of Mary), *True Devotion to Mary,* ch. 1, art. 2.

✛

The Little Book of
the Blessed Virgin Mary

Editor's note: The biblical quotations in the following pages are taken from the Douay-Rheims edition of the Old and New Testaments. Where applicable, quotations have been cross-referenced with the differing names and enumeration in the Revised Standard Version, using the following symbol: (RSV =).

Book I

The price of Mary's motherhood

The Glories of Mary and *The Splendors of Mary* are favorite titles. We seldom think of the Madonna without immediately calling to mind the fullness of her privileges, and too often perhaps slight meditation on the sublime sacrifices they entailed.

The word that most aptly summarizes the whole career of Mary is *mother.* Mother she is, and doubly so in the terms of Catholic belief: human Mother of Jesus, supernatural Mother of every Christian. Jesus, her Firstborn, she brought forth without pain; but in giving birth to her second-born, ah, what agony did she not have to endure! *In dolore paries*[6] has been said in the beginning. Every childbirth means suffering, but Mary, chosen by God that she might in Jesus Christ bring men to divine life, had to struggle with anguish proportionate to her extraordinary maternity.

In dolore paries; suffering, the price of motherhood! We ought to weigh well at what price Mary became the Mother of the human race.

---

[6] Gen. 3:16: "In sorrow shalt thou bring forth."

Chapter One

Mary is serene even in her sufferings

The sorrowful career of Mary dates, we might say, from the Purification. What Christian soul does not remember the tragic words of aged Simeon to the young mother who had come to offer her Son in the Temple? *A sword of sorrow will pierce your heart.*[7]

According to Jewish custom, women came to the Temple a few weeks after the birth of a child to present their offspring to the Lord. Mary conformed to this law.

Simeon, moved by the Spirit of God, went to the Temple. He knew, as did all the Jews, that the Messiah was near; he had, moreover, received a revelation that he would not die before he had seen the Redeemer of Israel. And now the hour in which he could contemplate Him had come.

See, in truth, the Anointed of the Lord . . .

Over there, under the porticos, stands a young mother and a man carrying two doves; the young mother holds her newborn

[7] Cf. Luke 2:35.

Babe close within her mantle. *Salutare Dei* — the Salvation of God! It is He! The frail Nothing within this tender nest is the Strength of God, *Salutare Dei*. This little bright spot in the protecting shadow is the Light that is to dissipate the darkness of the nations.

Here at last is *that hour* Simeon had been waiting for all his life. From his lips rises the hymn of thanksgiving: *Nunc dimittis servum tuum, Domine:* "Now, Lord, Thou dost dismiss Thy servant, for my eyes have seen Him whom all have so ardently desired!"[8]

Mary advances, holding her treasure, and Simeon, with clumsy hands, receives the Infant from her. Jesus feels, indeed, that He loses by the change; this is not the gentle embrace of the Virgin. He thinks of other arms, arms that later on will treat Him in a rougher fashion. The man of God raises toward the Lord this dear little one, a Victim marked for sacrifice, and then, the offering made, gives back the precious bundle to the young mother.

Under the action of divine inspiration, what does he say to that Mother, thrilled by the offering to which, with all her love, she unites herself? What does he say? Caressing words? Enchanting words?

No, indeed, terrifying words: "This little one, O Mother, *will be a sign for contradiction*, that is to say, humanity on His account will be divided; some will be for Jesus Christ, and others will be against Him, and these latter, alas, will succeed in killing Him. As for you, poor woman, *a sword of sorrow will pierce your heart*; in other words: judge by what is awaiting Jesus, what is in store for His Mother; measure your affliction by the tribulations of your Son. You will be to coming generations the woman whose heart was pierced by the sword of incessant martyrdom . . . And now, if it is possible for you,

---

[8] Cf. Luke 2:29-30.

go in peace, and may the joy of the Savior remain with you." Ah, after such a prophecy, how could the heart of Mary refrain from tears? We call this a joyful mystery. Is it not rather an appallingly *tragic* mystery?

Here is the young mother. She is radiant in the first flush of maternal happiness; she cradles in her loving arms the sweet little life that throbs against her breast; suddenly with cruel frankness, not admitting the shadow of doubt or uncertainty, someone bends over her existence and that of her child and thrusts into her heart this frightful prophecy: "For Him, contradiction; for you, the sword. For Him, the Cross; for you, the foot of the Cross."

The Virgin was ignorant of nothing regarding the promised Messiah. She knew the Scriptures; she had meditated long on Isaiah and the prophets.

But what did Isaiah and the prophets foretell of the Messiah? The texts are marked with blood. Like Mary, we know them, but we know less well how to read them and how to ponder them. *"He will be a Man of Sorrows,* struck by God and humiliated because He will bear our infirmities. He will be pierced because of our sins, for Jehovah will let fall upon Him the iniquity of us all. From the sole of His feet to the crown of His head, He will be one wound."[9]

By gathering all the texts of the Old Testament that deal with the Savior, we can find a prophetic recital of the Passion down to the last detail, including the sponge, the gall, the vinegar, and the seamless robe for which lots were cast at the foot of the gibbet. Mary had read all and meditated on it all. She was under no delusion. God had most probably given her, by infused grace, some special light on the events that awaited her Son.

[9] Cf. Isa. 1:6; 53:3-5.

Man of Sorrows: that title is far from telling the whole story. In the involuntary brutality of vision, Isaiah spared no cruel details, summarizing his prophecy in these words: *No, not even the appearance of a man, a worm of the earth. Man of sorrows! One wound! A worm of the earth!* Thus spoke the great prophet, and Mary holds all these words in her heart.

But today it is no longer a question of texts, of words rising out of the depths of the ages whose distant mists shade off somewhat their too-sharp outlines. *A sword, O Mary, will pierce your heart!* Mary hears the frightening prophecy, and nothing dulls its keen edges.

This Son, O Mother, will indeed be the Messiah of suffering described by Holy Scripture.

The better to understand Mary's position, let us transpose the case to a modern situation. Twenty years before the war, a young mother bends over the cradle of her child. Someone, with the absolute certainty of a true prophet approaches her, saying, "Listen, O Mother. I shall describe to you in advance the events of your little one's future and the circumstances of his death. Summon all your courage, for your poor little one will die alone, stretched out on the field of battle, his body riddled, his head on fire, calling to you in the night."

What a heartbreak for a woman thus forewarned! Ordinarily, mothers are happy in thinking of their newborn babes just because they do not know their future; they do not know what will come to their offspring. A mother, we say, weaves golden dreams for her child.

For Mary, there are no golden dreams, but clear prevision tinged with blood. This little one whom the tender old man gives back to her keeping is destined for martyrdom, and Mary will live, or rather, will die throughout thirty-three years in the anguish of this thought: *My Son is a future crucified!*

She is at home again. Simeon has given her back her Child. Poor Mary! Her mission of mother is to rear Him for the sacrifice. She is to prepare the Victim for the hour of the sword. That is her sole duty.

Thirteenth-century paintings of the Nativity generally have great theological significance. Some represent Mary, disconsolate, turning away from Jesus because she sees Him lying on an altar instead of in a crib; others picture Jesus turning away from Mary and her smile, because He perceives, in the heavens, angels who show Him the Cross and the other instruments of His Passion.

Let us endeavor to picture to ourselves the actual life of the Child and the Mother. See Jesus as a Babe on Mary's lap. Mary smiles contentedly while playing with the Infant, but suddenly a cloud passes before her eyes; distress grips her heart. Another day, as at this moment, she will again hold Him on her lap. Poor Mother! In thirty-three years, she will be at the foot of the gibbet; she will be the *Pietà*.

Away with this too-cruel perspective! She leans over the little one with greater love and kisses Him on the forehead. Then comes the harrowing thought: "In thirty-three years, instead of *my* kiss, He will receive the kiss of the thorns and the bloody pressure of the crown."

As He grows older, Mary can, with a caress, change into a smile the shadows that flit across His forehead or linger in His questioning but all-knowing eyes. She deludes herself into thinking that He is forgetting . . . that, for an instant, His divine knowledge fails Him and that He no longer thinks of two beams raising their sinister threat in the form of a cross against the horizon.

It had not always been easy to snatch the little one from peril. Even as a babe, He had wished to play with the Cross . . . and the persecution of Herod had sprung up. The Innocents had been massacred, but He, *the Innocent,* had escaped. It was a drawn game. One day, evil would be conqueror. How many times in thinking of the two arms of the gibbet, the Virgin clasped her infant more lovingly to her breast!

One day, yes, one day, the two arms of the cross would triumph over the two arms of the woman. And Mary's embrace grew more tender as if to compensate in advance for the odious embrace of the wood of death.

A famous painting represents Jesus in the workshop of Joseph. The Child, as the center of interest, carries on His shoulder two beams that throw on the white wall behind Him the tragic symbol of an anticipated Golgotha; the Mother, seated in the corner among the yellow shavings, does not turn toward Jesus standing in the foreground, but toward the wall on which the two beams cast their shadow dramatically prophetic. A true picture, for every time Mary looked at Jesus, she could see silhouetted behind Him the menace of the gibbet; the Cross, frightful sign, placed at the prominent point of the *country of contradiction.*

Catholic piety is not mistaken in calling Mary the Queen of Martyrs, for, as Mother of a Son like Jesus, not only did her sorrow surpass every other sorrow in intensity, but her anguish of soul was beyond all other anguish in its duration.

From the arms of Simeon to the arms of the Cross, Jesus lived thirty-three years: thirty-three years of suffering for Mary. We include all the sorrows of Mary under the title Our Lady of Seven Dolors, because on seven notable occasions more memorable than others, Mary particularly suffered: the Prediction of Simeon, the Flight into Egypt, the Loss in the Temple, the Meeting on the

Road to Calvary, the Three Hours on Calvary, the Taking Down from the Cross, and the Burial. But the title Our Lady of Seven Dolors has a still deeper meaning; seven is a biblical figure indicating an immense number that defies count: the Virgin of Seven Sorrows, the Virgin Ever-Suffering.

From the Purification to Calvary, Mary was at each moment of her existence a prey to limitless sorrow; but she was never crushed, never without animation or spirit. A profound joy accompanied her at every instant; an invincible serenity suffused her personality.

What was the source of this joy and serenity if not her absolute and radiant acceptance of the Father's every wish? Like Jesus, she could say, "My meat is to do the will of the Father who is in Heaven,"[10] that is to say, "The divine will is the marrow of my existence, its very essence." Crucifying though this will might be for Mary, the happiness experienced in accomplishing it outstripped the sufferings involved; the breathing of Mary was like that of Jesus, a perpetual *Amen*, an unfailing *Yes, Father*. This complete conformity to all the wishes of God imparted to her a foretaste of beatitude against which nothing could prevail.

With what unparalleled joy, moreover, did not the thought of being the Mother of such a Son flood her soul. If every woman who brings a child into the world is transported with joy at the thought of her motherhood, what ecstasy must Mary have experienced in her privilege of being the Mother of God!

But this consideration of the perfect serenity of Mary, Mother of All Joy, Our Lady of Gladness, should not permit us to forget the agony of suffering ever present in her life. St. Alphonsus Liguori,

[10]Cf. John 4:34.

commenting on the sorrows of Mary, explains that hers was a martyrdom without consolation.[11] On the other hand, the English Oratorian Faber, stressing, rather, the serenity of Mary, affirms that at each instant, the Virgin was consoled in her sorrow. Both are right, but, instead of considering their views as contradictory, we must unite them.

The Savior, from the first moment of His entrance into human existence, had before His eyes the perspective of His Calvary. His divine knowledge unfolded for Him all the dreadful aspects of the agony: the odious conduct of the tribunals, the condemnation, the elevation on the Cross. At every instant, a horrible vision rose before Him, but at the same time He experienced, of necessity, the Beatific Vision.

When we see our Lord appearing transfigured in the Gospel, we must not conclude that only then did the Son of God benefit by that radiant life. Absolute happiness was His habitual state. Therefore, although it pleased Him to manifest His glory only partially, as in the Transfiguration, nevertheless, the glory invisible to us, but effective for Him in reality, never left Him. Similarly, when our Lord appears as a crushed victim in the agony, we must not conclude that only then was the Son of God broken by sorrow. Our Lord was in agony always, since, at each instant, His divine knowledge showed Him completely the future toward which He was advancing.

Present to Him always were the Mount of Olives and the Mount of Tabor: at each instant, heartbreak and joy, agony and the splendor of beatitude. In this consists one of the aspects, and

---

[11]St. Alphonsus Liguori (1696-1787; bishop, writer, and founder of the Redemptorists), *The Glories of Mary*, "Sermon on the Dolors of Mary."

not the least surprising, of Christ's two natures: the human and the divine in the unity of a single person.

The hypostatic union, of course, did not apply to the Blessed Virgin; that is self-evident. We can, nevertheless, compare the state of her soul with that of her Son. Perfectly enlightened about the future, she lived in a continual agony; perfectly submissive to God and profoundly happy in being the Mother of the Savior, she experienced ineffable joy. Mary, like her Son, lived Gethsemane and Tabor simultaneously. We must never let the thought of her Tabor make us forget her perpetual Gethsemane!

The Church keeps the memory of it for us. Although she does not give the feast commemorating Mary's sorrows the solemn rank of the Assumption or the Immaculate Conception, she has, by way of compensation, set aside two feasts in the liturgical year to honor our Lady's dolors.

The Feast of the Compassion of the Blessed Virgin, the Friday of Passion Week, dates from the beginning of the fifteenth century. It was inaugurated by the Archbishop of Cologne in 1423, as an honorable reparation for the outrages of the Hussites against the images of the Mother of God, particularly as the *Pietà*. At the end of the same century, in 1482, Pope Sixtus IV, the Franciscan and a brother in religion to Jacopone de Todi, the author of the *Stabat Mater*, extended it to the whole Church; and in 1725, Benedict XII raised it to the rank of a double major, giving it a fixed place in the liturgical calendar. The second Feast of the Sorrows of Mary is solemnized in September. Pope Pius VII, in gratitude to our Lady for having consoled him during the captivity to which the emperor Napoleon had subjected him, established it on the occasion of his deliverance, September 18, 1814.

The Legend of the Eighth Sword is an appealing story that we might well recall in considering Our Lady of Seven Dolors. A young man, accustomed to visit the Madonna each day, fell into sin. When he returned to the feet of the Virgin, he was surprised to find that one sword more than usual pierced the heart of the *Pietà*. He understood its significance immediately. Then and there, he sought a priest and made his confession, which snatched from the heart of his mother the newly thrust sword. Back again he went to the Madonna; the eighth sword had disappeared. This was indeed a touching symbol, expressive of a great idea.

Chapter Two

Mary fully accepts God's will

Although the Purification marks the feast of Mary's dolors, an exact account of her sufferings leads us back to that moment of moments in which she was informed of the part God wanted her to take in the great work of the Redemption of the Cross.

It sometimes happens that Good Friday falls on March 25, the Feast of the Annunciation. The occurrence, however, is not constant; but the two feasts are not far apart, for the anniversary of the angel's visit to Mary can never be separated from the cruel memory of the death of the Savior. The simultaneous commemoration of these two anniversaries is more than a simple coincidence. It is the concurrence of two feasts united by the closest bonds.

The tidings brought to Mary could not but bring to our Lady tragic perspectives.

Mary is at home praying — at home, in the little house of Joachim and Anna. The small dwelling composed of only two sections is built snugly into the side of the hill; Mary's own room is a recess in the rock covered by a slanting roof. It is in this secluded part of the house, the hollow in the rock, that the Annunciation takes place.

Written in letters of silver on the slab of stone that marks the sacred spot, the following words recall the sublime event of that celebrated March 25: *Hic de Maria Virgine, Verbum caro factum est* — "Here of the Virgin Mary, the Word was made flesh."

The house is rather poor, even though Mary is of the royal family of David; this noble family has lost its worldly prestige. She lives not in destitution exactly, but in extreme simplicity. The Son of God will have nothing to do with luxury.

The Virgin must be about fifteen or sixteen years old. For several months, she has been betrothed to Joseph the Carpenter,[12] and her days roll by in the anticipation of the great events for which preparations are being made. At this particular time, Mary is praying.

It is related that St. Louis,[13] upon arriving in the country of Christ, wished to make a pilgrimage to the house of Joachim and Anna, to this room in the rock where the Virgin had learned the great plans of God regarding her life. On March 24, 1251, he went there on foot, had the divine office celebrated, and communicated at the hand of the Legate on the very spot where, according to tradition, the angelic salutation had been pronounced.

Let us imitate good St. Louis. Let us go, in thought at least, to Mary's room and contemplate. What matters the habitation or the

---

[12]The principal dates of her life would be: the Annunciation: 15 years; the flight into Egypt: 17 years; the return to Nazareth: 22 years; the loss of the Child Jesus in the Temple: 27 years; the death of St. Joseph: 42 years (?); the departure of Jesus for His public life: 45 years; the Passion: 48 years; the death of Mary: 72 years.

[13]St. Louis IX (1214-1270), King of France.

site? It is the interior of the soul that attracts us. Let us penetrate reverently into this sanctuary, the Heart of Mary.

Several Fathers of the Church suggest the nature of the young Virgin's prayer before the visit of the angel. She is making an offering of herself, certainly not to become the Mother of the promised Messiah; her humility would never have dreamed of that. She is offering herself to be the handmaid of the woman blessed among all women whom God has chosen to become that privileged one.[14] For Mary realizes that the Messiah must be quite near. Like all the Jews of her time, she knows that the promised Redeemer will not delay, if indeed, He is not already on earth . . .

He is to be of Israel; there is no doubt about that. And, since Daniel's time, the date of His coming is in all minds. The seventy weeks of years announced by the prophet are coming to a close; the Messiah, for a certainty, is not far distant. When John the Baptist preached at the Jordan, did not the Jews, filled with the idea that the Redeemer was at hand, seek him out to determine if he was the Expected One, the Desired of the Nations? Among them, there is a difference on a single point only: some await the Messiah under the form of a temporal restorer of the kingdom of Zion; others, the pious Jews, who frequent the synagogue, look for the Messiah under the true form of spiritual Redeemer. But all are agreed upon the certainty of His immediate advent.

The Virgin belongs evidently to the instructed and pious Jews who expect the *true* Redeemer. He will have a mother; the sacred books announced that in formal terms. If only this mother, if this privileged woman be pleased to utilize the services of Mary of Nazareth — what joy!

[14]This supposition is a pure hypothesis. We say later that Mary knew the plan of God for her life.

Behold, suddenly a mysterious and radiant person enters. He bows reverently.

Hail, full of grace!

The Virgin arises . . .

The archangel continues: "The Lord is with thee . . . Blessed art thou among women";[15] that is to say: "There is no question of being the servant of her who is to be the blessed one. *You* are the chosen of God; *you* are the one the Lord has marked to be the Mother of the promised Redeemer."

As Gabriel sees that she to whom he is speaking is troubled, he reassures her: "Fear not, Mary!"

Again in other words he qualifies her as *benedicta*, blessed, she of whom it was said "the Most High has made her His consecrated one, His chosen one among the *daughters of Zion*."

"You have found grace with God";[16] that is to say, the Lord calls you by a signal mercy to a unique role.

The salutation will become still clearer when Mary hears the message:

> *Behold, you will conceive in your womb, and you will bring forth a Son, and you will call His Name Jesus. He will be great, He will be called the Son of the Most High. Of His kingdom there will be no end.*[17]

Now the light is complete. She can no longer doubt: it is an invitation to collaborate in the redemptive plan. The Messiah asks for a mother.

Mary, are you willing to be that mother?

[15]Luke 1:28.
[16]Luke 1:30.
[17]Luke 1:31-33.

A strange proposition, in truth! How interesting for us to know what Mary is going to answer, to discover the reaction that is hers at the decisive moment of this singular proposition, to penetrate to the depths of her sentiments at this hour when the whole future of humanity is at stake!

We are not indulging in simple conjectures; we have the recital of St. Luke, the Evangelist, who declares in unmistakable terms: "Mary was quite troubled"[18] by this singular offer. *Turbata est.*

And why is she astonished? She is troubled at first through humility. True, she is of noble lineage, even though the grandeur of the royal line of David is on the wane. But how could God have chosen her who is so unimportant, so hidden, for the Mother of the Redeemer? In this respect, Faber's observation is exact: "The mystery took her unawares, and until the moment came, the greatness of her knowledge and the wonder of her conscious holiness had not so much as excited a suspicion in her beautiful humility."[19] Therefore, before this astonishing proposition, she finds herself disconcerted for an instant; the angel, to reassure her, explains more fully the plan of God. She has found grace with Him by reason of her very littleness. Moreover, the conception will be entirely virginal; she will bring the Messiah into the world, but her motherhood will not be brought about by any human agent but, rather, through the operation of the Holy Spirit.

The angel recognizes that humility and her vow of virginity are the reasons for Mary's trouble and momentary hesitation, which necessitates his confirming explanations and words of comfort.

Is there not also a third motive? Mary knows thoroughly, as did every faithful Jew, the prophecies concerning the Messiah. She

---

[18]Luke 1:29.

[19]Frederick William Faber, *Bethlehem*, ch. 2.

knows that the Savior will buy back the world by an unprecedented sacrifice . . . The Mother of the Messiah, in her eyes, is not to be the mother of a conqueror covered with human glory, but of a reviled, derided King crowned with thorns. Is it possible that at the tidings of the angel, the whole future of wounds and blood does not surge into her thoughts? Is it possible that Mary enters into the Redemption without any knowledge of what it will cost her and her Son? No

Ought we not rather to suppose that God, to increase the merit of the Blessed Virgin and to avoid the reproach of having betrayed her into consent, gave her, in addition to the light she already possessed from the Scriptures, new light relevant to her mission and its responsibilities? It is difficult to believe that it could be otherwise. A close study of the story of the Annunciation as it is given by St. Luke lends more than a little weight to the plausibility of our explanation.

At first sight, in fact, we might imagine that confronted with the proposition of the angel, the spontaneous reaction of Mary, after recovering from her first surprise, must have been joy, an unmixed joy. Again, if we do not take the trouble to reflect sufficiently, we might be tempted to let the memorable words of Mary's *Magnificat*,[20] the most beautiful outburst of joy history ever recorded, the cry par excellence of perfect exultation, rise to our lips as expressive of her sentiments at this moment. Surely, at the Annunciation in response to the angel's message, Mary must have again given voice with full heart to her exultant song! There before her stands one who reveals to her that, by a mere consent, she can become the Mother of God! Oh, what happiness! *Magnificat! Magnificat!*

[20]Luke 1:46-55.

Such was not the case, however. The *Magnificat* does *not* date from this day. Search the Gospel text to find it. Listen to the word that Mary is to pronounce. A word of enthusiastic joy? Not at all. What does she say? "Fiat . . . I accept. Let it be done to me as God wills. I consent."

Fiat.

Fiat, "I consent"; and not *Magnificat*, "I exalt."

Fiat? I know that word; it is a word of agony. In thirty-three years, I shall hear Christ sigh it under the olive trees of Gethsemane: "Father, Father, take away this chalice! Nevertheless, Your will I accept, *fiat.*"[21]

Can there be in the exclamation of Mary some hint of frightful anguish? Without any doubt. There is no thought of the Blessed Virgin's entering into a redemptive plan that will cost her nothing. She is asked if she will consent to become the mother of a *future crucified*. Equivalently, then, she is being asked to become herself a *crucified*. And our Lady, capable in her love for God and for us of heroic courage, accepts and says: *"Fiat.* Someone is needed . . . Here I am. Behold! Self-sacrifice, devotion and service will be required? The Lord can count on me . . . *Ancilla*. Let it cost what the good God wills: all the blood of Jesus and all the tears of my mother-heart to bring Him to the moment of crucifixion, I accept, *fiat!*" Ah, how that word strikes the true note! *Magnificat* . . . that will be for another day! In this hour . . . *fiat! Fiat!*

On one of the walls of the Armenian cathedral of Lwow in Poland, Jan Jenryck Rosen, a pupil of Luc-Olivier Merson, has painted a very expressive Annunciation. In the foreground, the angel is saluting Mary; in the background, through the arches of a colonnade looms the hill of Calvary, which Jesus, weighed down

---

[21] Cf. Matt. 26:39.

with His Cross, is climbing, and behind Him, at some distance from a group of women, stands the grieving Madonna. Is it simply the fantasy of an artist that brings together these two mysteries? Not at all. It is rather the expression of a psychological truth.

The purpose of Christ's coming upon earth was to restore to men the divine life lost through Original Sin. The purpose of Mary's *fiat* was to make possible the realization of Christ's coming. Thus, the *ecce ancilla domini* ("Behold the handmaiden of the Lord") makes the Blessed Virgin doubly a mother: human Mother of Jesus according to the flesh, supernatural Mother of all redeemed human beings.

What would have happened if Mary had not consented? It is only a supposition, of course, made in the light of the knowledge that Mary actually did consent.[22] But it could have been otherwise. Mary was perfectly free. She accepted. Well and good! But if she had refused? It was, after all, in her power to do so.

Let us suppose that Mary, confronted with the dramatic intensity of the sorrowful future opening up before her, would have said that she was not able to assume such a charge. In truth, this refusal was possible. What would have come of it? There would be no Jesus the Redeemer, no Redemption, at least not by the means anticipated. In consequence, the divine life lost in the beginning

[22]Terrien, in his excellent works on the question — *Marie, Mère de Dieu, Marie, Mère des Hommes*, Vol. 3, Bk. 2, ch. 3 — shows very clearly how the freedom of Mary's consent did not compromise the realization of the divine plan. Berulle observes that Mary's consent makes her the most remarkable *personality* in the world. In our Lord, nature alone seems to be honored, since the person of Christ is divine. In Mary, the person is glorified as no other has ever been before.

would not have been restored to us; we would have been forever deprived of the supernatural — and Mary, through one act, would have escaped the whole career of the *Dolorosa*.

She accepted, we know. There would be a Redeemer, then a Redemption; the forfeited divine life would be restored to us. The consent of Mary is the origin of a double birth: Christ's birth and ours. But at what price such nativities!

The Nativity of Jesus is a familiar subject to us. Let us now consider especially our own. We often say, "Mary is our Mother." Do we understand well the deep significance of this word? Do we understand that, at a given moment in the history of the world, the salvation of our entire humanity depended on the modest response that this youthful Mary was to make in this little hamlet of Galilee? Do we understand that the *fiat* coming from her lips is a heroic *fiat*? Do we understand that it was, without doubt, love of God and also love for mankind that gave Mary the courage to accept? Do we realize the extent of her love for both? Nothing gives us a better idea of it than to compare the conduct of Mary with that of the thrice-holy Father and the Son, the Word Incarnate. Mary, with all the fullness of perfection of which she is capable, forms her attitude in close imitation of theirs.

What is the attitude of the Son of God in this divine history of souls? Let us consider Him as the Word and try to elevate ourselves in thought to that period of eternity preceding the Incarnation. We could picture Him in His relation to the Father in the bosom of the Trinity; but that does not suit our purpose here. We will rather picture the Word in His relation to us and to our Redemption. To do this, we must go back into the depths of eternity, where we will find the Word, that incomparable Person, occupied in thinking of us, in offering Himself for us, in meditating on that prodigious Incarnation that will make Him one of us.

The author of the letter to the Hebrews represents the Word declaring, upon His entrance into the world, "*Ecce venio* — Behold, I come."[23] The *ecce* pronounced at this moment was but an echo of the Word's eternal utterance throughout the length of the infinite present which is the proper life of God. The Word, with us in mind, delivered Himself up completely to all that He and the Father and the Holy Spirit had decided, thus living in advance the hour fixed by divine decree.

In the beautiful contemplation of the Incarnation in the *Spiritual Exercises*, St. Ignatius of Loyola[24] imagines a sort of council of the Holy Trinity, a deliberation of the three divine Persons, to decide what was proper to do in the face of the eternally previsioned Fall of the first human couple, and of its sinister consequences.

No reparation of an exclusively human order would suffice. There was an infinite character to the Fall. How could man left to himself ever furnish an infinite reparation? The Word, then, would descend among us on the appointed day. He would take a body like ours, live with us for thirty-three years, and finally die upon the Cross. This, then, is the eternal action of the Word, the offering of Himself for us. It is He, the Word, who eternally renews His act of immolation. Someone is needed. *Ecce venio.* Someone to sacrifice Himself? *I shall be that Someone. Ecce venio.*

On the appointed day, He came. In Heaven, He could give to His Father only the homage of an equal to an equal. In becoming incarnate, that is, in taking a body like ours, He made Himself *inferior*. He would be able to obey, to do the will of One greater than He — thus, in the whole strength of the word, to serve. What had been decided in common He would realize alone.

---

[23] Heb. 10:7.

[24] St. Ignatius of Loyola (1491-1556), founder of the Jesuit Order.

Ecce Puer ("Behold a Child") . . . The years rolled by — the Passion began. Pilate led Christ forth. *Ecce homo* ("Behold the Man") . . . But that was not all. The Word was made *flesh*. He was made one wound. He became *bread* to remain always in the Eucharist, where, as in the Passion, the same word expresses His profound attitude of immolation. Behold, I offer myself, I give myself . . . *Ecce Agnus Dei* ("Behold the Lamb of God")!

Look at Mary . . . What answer does she give the angel who asks her if she is willing to serve, to consent to a sacrificial collaboration in the great work of the Redemption? A single word, exactly the same as that of the Son: *Ecce* . . . Is it a question of giving myself? I understand, I am ready. I offer myself, I devote myself to serve. *Ecce, Ancilla!*

It is impossible to represent more perfectly the substantial attitude of the Word, of the Word Incarnate. No creature has ever been more truly *another Christ*, more truly a *Christian* than Mary, the Mother of Christ.

If she imitated and reproduced perfectly the attitude of the Son, she likewise imitated and reproduced perfectly the Father's love for us. What was the plan of the Father? To save us through the sacrifice of His Son. A prodigy unheard of, but an unquestionable reality! The Father saw before Him two classes of children: His only-begotten Son, the Well-beloved Word, All-Wisdom, All-Purity, whom He encompasses with an infinite complacence, and from whom He receives a filial love without measure; and us, His adopted children, who, by the ancestral Fall, became sad rebels, with meanness and stupidity our most eminent prerogatives, possessing nothing that merits complacence and manifesting very little concern about loving the Father.

Strange though it may seem, the Father, in dealing with His two classes of children — the Only-Begotten and the adopted

Sons; the One without spot, the others tainted; the One, the infinite Word, the others, weak nothings and rebellious — seemed to favor the second, to prefer them to the first. Salvien, a sacred author, remarks, "God seems to have loved His adopted sons more than His only-begotten Son; His culpable children more than the Word of all Purity, since to save them, He accepted the sacrifice of His Firstborn."

Ah, we speak of the folly of the Son, the folly of the Cross, but the folly of the Father's love, what do we not say of that? What a prodigy! "God so loved the world that He gave His only-begotten Son!"[25] To such an extent has the Father loved the world, since, to restore it to the divine life it had lost, He accepted for His Son the crib, the thirty-three years on earth, the death on the Cross! The Father has loved *even to that!*

Such, too, was the extent of Mary's love. Her situation in face of the message of the angel resembles that of the Father. She also has two classes of children: her Son and us. The proposal made to her is this: to sacrifice her Firstborn to save us, to consent to bring Him into the world in order to yield Him up to the Cross. As the Father preferred us to His only-begotten Son, so, too, did Mary prefer us to her Jesus. It was our interest that took precedence in the moment of her great decision. If she said *yes*, Jesus would be condemned but mankind would be saved; if she said *no*, Jesus would escape, but humanity would remain fallen.

And Mary said, "Yes, *fiat.*"[26]

How truly little Guy de Fontgalland spoke when he said, "The nicest word to say to the good God is yes!" Had the Blessed Virgin

[25]John 3:16.

[26]In thinking of this yes, St. Augustine (354-430; Bishop of Hippo) calls Mary *Causa libertatis*, "the cause of our liberty."

not said it to the angel of the Incarnation, what would have become of the world?

We can carry our examination of the consequences of the *Ecce Ancilla Domini* still farther.

To save us, the Word of God was not content to become man like us and to die for us. He wished to unite Himself to us, to incorporate us, or, as St. Paul says, to identify[27] us with Himself: "I am the Vine, you are the branches."[28] The complete Christ was not only to be Jesus the individual, the Child of the Father, and the Son of the Virgin, but Jesus *plus* all men vitally grafted upon Him by sanctifying grace.

Herein we find the reason for the expressions the *Only-Begotten* and the *Firstborn*. Jesus is both the one and the other. He is par excellence the only Son; He is equally the eldest of many brothers, the Head of the whole line of the elect who will be saved only in Him and through Him. Jesus did not come to earth to be the only Son, for He had been that for eternity, since He was the eternal Son of the Father. It was rather to be the *Firstborn* that the Word became incarnate, to incorporate with Himself all His heavenly Father's previously adopted children, deprived by Original Sin of their divine life. Jesus had no other aim than to unite humanity to His Father by first uniting it to Himself. The redeemed would be redeemed only so far as they would be one with Christ,

---

[27]Father Prat: "The Mystery par excellence is the plan, conceived by God from all eternity but revealed only in the Gospel, of saving all men by identifying them with His Well-Beloved Son in the unity of the Mystical Body," *La Theologie de saint Paul*, 15th ed., Vol. I, 369.

[28]John 15:5.

incorporated with His Person in the unity of a single whole, a single Body. Jesus was made man only to be the Head, the Chief of the great Body, to assimilate to Himself all humanity.

From then on, the maternity of Mary assumes a singular fullness. Do not these lines from Louis de Montfort give us much to think about: "If Jesus Christ, the Head of men, was born in her, the predestinate who are the members of that Head, ought also to be born in her as a necessary consequence. One and the same Mother does not bring forth into the world the head without its members, nor the members without the head, for this would be a monster of nature. Likewise, in the order of grace, the head and the members are born of one and the same Mother; and if a member of the Mystical Body of Jesus Christ — that is to say, one of the predestinate — were born of another mother than Mary, who has produced the Head, he would not be one of the predestinate, nor a member of Jesus Christ, but simply a monster in the order of grace."[29]

We do not pretend at all that Mary is the Mother of the Mystical Body — that is, of the members of Christ — *in the same manner* and *in the same sense* that she is the Mother of the Divine Head, Jesus, our Lord. In His case, she is mother according to nature; in the case of the members, she is mother according to grace. It is an essential difference. Besides, when we consider the role of mother played by Mary relative to the Mystical Body, we must not forget that the Virgin is herself a part of the Mystical Body; that she is, like us, an adopted daughter of God; that, strictly speaking, it is not she who gives life to the members of Christ, but the Holy Spirit, who, by His supernatural indwelling in each one, is the only source of that grace which is at the same time in Christ, in Mary, and in all the faithful. Mary is the Mother of the Mystical

[29]Louis de Montfort, *True Devotion to Mary*, ch. 1, art. 3.

Body only in the sense that, by her obedience to God, she rendered possible such great mysteries and that, by her merits, she contributes with the saints to the growth of that supernatural organism, as we shall explain later.

This having been said, it still remains that Mary, in consenting to become the Mother of Christ, was not ignorant of the fact that her maternity was to be different in that it concerned at the same time our Lord and us; in other words, that it was not merely a question of accepting only the motherhood of Jesus, but of becoming the Mother of the complete Jesus, of the great and entire Jesus Christ, the Head and the members.

Would it be fitting to separate Jesus from His brethren, the body from the members? We do not think so. Jesus came only to be the Firstborn; expressly to give sons to His heavenly Father by identifying humanity with Himself. He had no other reason for being than to unite humanity to His Father by uniting it to Himself. For our part, we side willingly with the judgment of a solid and pious author: "There did not exist in Jesus a private character and a public character; Christ existed wholly for His mission." Thus is explained the maternity of Mary in relation to men. She is Mother of Christ, who is the Head of humanity, and of Christ in His members, who can have supernatural being only through oneness with Christ.

We cannot, then, separate Mary, the Mother of God, from Mary, the Mother of men. Jesus is inseparable from His brethren, existing only for them; and she is the Mother of the elder Brother solely that she might give birth to His brethren according to the spirit. Thus, in consenting to become the Mother of Jesus, she consented by the same act to be the Mother of those who were to be a part of the Mystical Body."[30]

[30]Bainvel, *Marie, Mère de Grace* (Beauchesne, 1921).

If it is true that we cannot separate Jesus from His brethren, the Body from its members, we cannot separate in Mary her role of Mother of God and her role of Mother of men. She is Mother of the whole Jesus, the physical body and the Mystical Body; of the physical body of Jesus by her blood, of the Mystical Body of Jesus by her free consent and by her love. Mother of the one by nature, of the other by gracious consent, she began from the moment of her *fiat* to carry and to nourish in her heart full of love the children of men, as she began to carry and to nourish in her womb the Word of God.[31]

Pius X writes:

Is not Mary the Mother of Christ? She is, then, also our Mother; that is why we who are united to Jesus Christ and as says Saint Paul (Eph. v, 30), "who are members of His body, of His flesh and of His bones," have come forth from the womb of Mary as a body united to its head. From whence it follows that in a spiritual and mystical sense, we are called the children of Mary, and she is our Mother. Spiritual Mother, certainly, but nevertheless the true Mother of the members of Christ; and we are truly her children.[32]

---

[31] *Ita, ex tunc, omnes in suis visceribus bajulat, sicut verissima Mater, filios suos* (St. Anselm [c. 1033-1109; Archbishop of Canterbury]).

[32] *Ad diem illum*, February 22, 1904.

Chapter Three

Mary unites her sufferings with Christ's

There are those who imagine that, for Mary, the ascent of Calvary lasted only a single hour, fifty or sixty minutes at the end of Good Friday morning! They do not measure rightly.

For the Virgin, the climb to Calvary began at the infancy of Jesus. It is clearly evident that Mary knew she was rearing her Child for sacrifice. Can a mother who knows the sorrowful future of her child be other than a *Dolorosa*?

The apprehension of an ordeal is one thing; its realization is quite another.

The days passed, each one bringing Mary closer to that grim Friday which was to see her Son die. The slender pine which would soon lend its branches for the Cross had already been cut down. The acacia branches that would soon provide the crown of thorns stood ready. It was Thursday evening; the death on the Cross would be tomorrow — tomorrow at the ninth hour.

How did the Blessed Virgin learn of the arrest of her divine Son? We do not know. She most probably heard it through one of the apostles in flight or through a public rumor. "Have you heard the news? They have arrested Him!" *They* — that is to say, the enemies of the Savior, the Savior who spoke words of peace, who wished only good to all. There were whispered reports on all sides of the treason of one of the Twelve, of the kiss in the darkness, of Peter unsheathing his sword, of the scattered flight of the little group who had been faithful until then. Rumor was added to rumor. "They came with torches and sticks, and they have taken Him and led Him away!" . . . Perhaps someone, in order to console the poor Mother, added, "Don't be afraid; His innocence is bound to be justified."

Kindhearted people they were, but they suspected nothing of the future. They were afraid, but of what, they did not know. Mary was ignorant of nothing. She knew what was to come only too well. But perhaps her maternal love forced itself to hope against all hope. *They* had tried before to seize Him and to do Him harm. The hour had not come. Had the hour sounded this time? Alas, how could she doubt it?

What a night the poor Mother of the Savior, Jesus, must have passed after the events of such an evening! From hour to hour, news from the different tribunals arrived. If she had for a moment hesitated to believe, she could do so no longer; she had the evidence that, before the Crucifixion, had crucified her.

Was the Virgin able to follow these tragic meetings to which our Lord was dragged, to be derided, condemned? We do not know; the Gospel says nothing. Was she in the square, at the foot of the balcony of Antonia, when Pilate led Christ forth to the crowd? It is more than likely.

"No reason for condemnation," the Procurator had declared. "I find nothing to punish in this man." Nothing to punish! And he ordered the chastisement of slaves to be inflicted upon Him! It was necessary to appease the excited mob; this crowd would not have the deplorable courage to demand death for an unfortunate man, drenched with blood, crowned with thorns!

What short-visioned psychology! The cries burst out: "To death! To death! Crucify Him!" And there, in a retreat of the wall, surrounded by some friends, the Mother of the condemned can see her Son.

"Behold your victim, O Jews, there He is! Are you not satisfied now? *Ecce Homo!*" Alas, no! That does not suffice at all. Nothing less than crucifixion will satisfy.

"Ah, this is indeed the hour of which He spoke to me," murmurs Mary to herself. "With His filial delicacy, He knew well how to soften the harrowing details so as not to cause me too much pain whenever we talked about the future. He hid much from me, but I understood all, and now I can no longer doubt. Suffering is necessary, then, to save the world! All-Holy Father, have pity! But since, with the offering of the Son, *Ecce Homo*, that of the Mother is required, take my suffering, *Ecce ancilla!*"

Jesus is condemned. The execution will allow no delay. The beams of the gibbet are already at hand. But a few minutes, and the procession of crucifixion is to start for Golgotha.

John approaches: "Oh, Mother, do not go! You will suffer too much. Remain. Why do you wish to be present at this tragedy? What good will your presence be? It will only make Him and you suffer more."

"My son, I must!"

Mary, the sorrowful Mother, must be near Jesus, the sorrowful Son.

Ah, when He passed through the villages healing, when He taught the crowds at the edge of the lake, when He fed the five thousand in the desert, or when Jerusalem acclaimed Him, Mary did not have to be present. Now that Jesus is suffering, His Mother must be near Him.

"John, my son, let us go."

The two, followed by a few women, force their way through some side streets to join the head of the procession. At a crossway, the group stops; they can hear the noise increase as the procession mounts the hill. At last, it comes in sight and there, there is Jesus!

Far in advance, a centurion carries at the end of his lance the piece of parchment upon which is written the name of the condemned. The street is narrow, and Mary can decipher the awkwardly scrawled letters: *Jesus of Nazareth, King of the Jews.*

Jesus! Bethlehem comes back to her; the joy and the anguish of the waiting, Christmas, the stable and the manger, the shepherds and the kings from the East, the massacre of Herod, Egypt, the life in exile, the return . . . Oh, yes, it had not always been easy to preserve the Child from danger. The wicked had cunningly laid their snares, but she had detected the very shadow of their threat. Alas, He was not always to escape! In vain had she tried. Today, He has fallen into their hands.

Jesus of Nazareth! . . . Nazareth! . . . That life apparently so calm, yet charged with apprehension, seemed but yesterday. There in the workshop of Joseph, the Son and the Mother had prepared themselves in silence for the great sacrifice . . . Ah, how she remembered those long intimate evenings with their delightful interchange of confidences, the trip to Jerusalem at the end of His childhood, the crushing loss climaxed by the statement apparently so harmless: "Before all, my Father's business."[33] Did she not continually ponder in her heart this tragic announcement? She lived on it. Each day, she seemed to die from it.

[33]Cf. Luke 2:49.

Today the harmless appearances are unmasked. In all its bloody reality the redemptive plan moves forward. The divine will of the Father, ratified eternally by the Son, demands accomplishment. The hour has come. What is the centurion carrying at the end of his lance if not the petition that delivers humanity — the title that executes Jesus and that has executed her all her life?[34]

King of the Jews — or rather, King of the human race. Poor King! How they have made Him expiate and pay dearly for His royalty!

Here He is exactly as she had pictured Him . . . Above the tops of the helmets, she follows the movement of an oblique beam jerking feverishly, as its victim stumbles along beneath it. Christ is that Victim! She does not see Him yet. But her heart goes faster and farther than her eyes. Poor, poor, well-beloved Son!

"Come," murmurs John. "Let us go away. You must not stay here."

"My place is here."

Jesus has ascended the hill and is close to His Mother. Now the heartbroken Mother can contemplate her child. *A King!* He has a crown! The pearls are the color of blood!

"Poor Mother, do not look. Turn away!"

But wait, what is this movement in the crowd? Who is that woman? She breaks through the barrier of the soldiers. She reaches Jesus. She holds out to Him a cloth. She wipes away the spittle and blood.

Veronica, compassionate and courageous Veronica, be blessed for your gesture of ardent pity, for your loving compassion.[35] "Veronica,

---

[34] Col. 2:14: "Blotting out the handwriting of the decree that was against us which was contrary to us. And He hath taken over the same out of the way, fastening it to the Cross."

[35] A holy grandmother was once explaining the Way of the Cross to her grandchild. After the explanation of the Sixth Station, the

it is the Mother of the condemned who blesses you! Veronica, for Him and for me, oh, thank you!"

Mary follows the procession. Guided by John and the women, she climbs the hill. Sculptors and artists of the thirteenth century often represented the Virgin carrying the Cross instead of the Cyrenean . . . There is a beautiful theology in this faulty history.

Calvary at last! The Cross is thrown to the ground. The soldiers seize Jesus. They pull off His clothing and brutally shove Him down upon the rough wood. They must work fast. Each is at his post; here are the nails, here the hammers. Get started!

Mary is there, she sees, and she hears . . . She sees the arm of her Jesus stretched savagely by a soldier, while others hold His legs. Now, in its turn, the other arm . . . She hears the dull noise of the nail pushing through the flesh under the strokes of the hammer, then the more resounding sound of the nail entering the wood. She sees the cords bind the limbs of the sacred body to the gibbet so that the wounds do not tear open.

Then the soldiers seize the Cross as they would seize a ladder that they wish to raise. It is heavy — these two beams that hold the body of a hanging man. Then come the frightful jolts. Tears and blood again ravage the sacred face. Veronica, O gentle woman, come to His aid! But, no, it is impossible to break through the guards; the soldiers maintain the line. All must keep at a distance.

The foot of the gibbet touches the edge of the hole prepared for it. It slips with a terrific jolt; a few supports, a little earth, and it is finished! The apparatus of death, the instrument of the redemption is raised. Then the soldiers permit the women to approach.

little one declared, "Wait a minute, Grandma, wait!" "What for, my little one?" "I am going to get my prettiest handkerchief to wipe the face of Jesus. Jesus will work His miracle for me, too. I love Him as much as Veronica."

Mary comes to the foot of the gibbet to share the three hours of agony. When, in the desert of Beersheba, Hagar saw her son Ishmael tortured by thirst and on the point of dying, she did not have the heart to stay near him. *Non videdo morientem filium*[36]: "No, I cannot be present at the death of my child." She stretched him out at the foot of a tree and went about a stone's throw away.

Mary does just the opposite. At the foot of the Cross, she has a mission. She must give to immolation, in whose spirit she has lived since the Annunciation, its last consecration, its full significance. All her life she has reared Jesus for the sacrifice. The sacrifice is to be consummated. She must see it through to the end.

Crucifixa . . . Crucifixum. To the crucified Mother belongs the duty of offering to God her crucified Son!

All His life, Jesus was on the cross.[37] So, too, was Mary, His Mother. But this is no longer the expectation; today marks the accomplishment. Formerly the dread of apprehension; today the agony of execution: there is indeed a difference. The actuality is above her prevision. Her whole life was on the cross, but the cross is still harder than the whole of her life!

It must be so, however. Therefore, Mary, during the three hours, stands at the foot of the bloody Trellis where the Living Vine is dying. "At the foot of the cross," objects St. Bernard.[38] "Do you believe that it was at the foot of the Cross? No, no, it is not *near* the cross that Mary is found, but *on* the cross,[39] nailed to its beams as Jesus is." "Look at Jesus," says St. Bonaventure, "countless wounds

---

[36]Gen. 21:16.

[37]*Tota vita Christi, crux et martyrium fuit.*

[38]St. Bernard (1090-1153), Abbot of Clairvaux.

[39]*Ubi stabas? Numquid juxta crucem? Imo et in cruce.*

line His body, but they unite into a single and unspeakable wound, in the Heart of Mary."[40]

According to the estimation of St. Bernadine of Siena,[41] her sorrow was such that if perchance it had been divided among all creatures capable of suffering, all would have immediately expired. "God did not permit this immense sorrow to kill the Virgin," he continues, "only because her hour had not yet come."

In virtue of Mary's fearful suffering, certain debatable traditions of art stressing, perhaps, the idea of some Fathers of the Church, represent Mary fainting at the foot of the Cross, as, for example, *Our Lady of the Agony*, by Raphael. Newman, in his volume *Devotion to the Blessed Virgin*, condemns the opinion of the three Doctors, St. Basil, St. Cyril, and St. John Chrysostom,[42] who were not unwilling to believe that Mary abandoned herself on Calvary to the torment of doubt. In 1580, Molanus, the celebrated Latin author of the *History of Religious Paintings and Pictures*, faithful to the intentions of the Council of Trent (session 25, ch. II), insisted vigorously that in the representations of Mary at the foot of the Cross, everything falsely pathetic should be suppressed. Theological science is unanimous in upholding this attitude which Pope Benedict XIV confirmed by strict command. Gibieuf, a well-known Oratorian in the seventeenth century, summarized general opinion in these words: "On Calvary, Mary was neither prostrate,

[40]*Singula vulnera, per ejus corpus dispersa, in uno corde sunt unita* (St. Bonaventure [1221-1274; Franciscan mystical theologian and scholastic, writer, and bishop]).

[41]St. Bernadine of Siena (1380-1444), Franciscan friar whose powerful preaching helped reform fifteenth-century society.

[42]St. Basil the Great (c. 329-379), Bishop of Cappadocia; possibly St. Cyril of Jerusalem (c. 315-386) or St. Cyril of Alexandria (c. 376-444), bishops; St. John Chrysostom (c. 347-407), Archbishop of Constantinople.

nor swooning, nor in any disposition which betrayed weakness; but upright and well on her feet."

Furthermore, a definite sentiment dominated her sorrow, an entire submission of her whole being to the redeeming wills of the Father and of her Son, motivated by her immense love for us, which made her accept, as the Father accepted, the sacrifice of His *firstborn* Son in order that we, His other sons, might be saved.

Gerson even goes so far as to say that Mary's love for us was so great, the harmonization of her soul with the will of God so complete, her knowledge of the necessity of the sacrifice of Jesus for the salvation of humanity so certain, that should Jesus in His atrocious agony have become detached from the redeeming wood, the Virgin, with her own hands, would have helped to fix Him there again. *Si Deus jussisset, crucifixisset.*

We might consider Gerson extreme, but we will surely agree with St. Francis de Sales:

Consider how love draws all the pains, all the torments, all the sufferings, all the sorrows, the wounds, the Passion, the Cross, and even the death of our Redeemer into the heart of His most Holy Mother. Alas, the same nails that crucify this divine Child crucify also the heart of the Mother; the same thorns which pierce His head pierce the soul of that most gentle Mother. Through her condolence, she had the same sorrows that her Son suffered; the same passions through compassion, in a word, the sword of death which pierced the Body of this well-beloved Son likewise pierced the heart of that most loving Mother, inasmuch as the heart of the Mother was one with her Son in so perfect a union that nothing could wound the one without also wounding the other. Her maternal breast thus wounded by love, far from seeking the cure of her wound, loved it more than any heal-ing, cherishing the marks of sorrow that love had engraved on her heart, and desiring continually to die of this wound, since her Son had died of it amid the flames of charity, a perfect holocaust for all the sins of the world.[43]

"It was not in vain," comments the saintly blind prelate Monsi-gnor de Ségur, "that Jesus Christ wished Mary to stand at the foot of His Cross, and that she is shown to us there present at His death as a great witness of the divinity of the Blood He pours out for the salvation of the world. The cross leans thus upon Mary as much as Mary leans upon the Cross ... 'Take away Mary and the cross falls,' said Saint Cyril at the ecumenical Council at Ephesus. The Virgin brought forth without pain the thrice-holy Christ. Now that her Son and her God has accomplished His mission upon earth, she brings forth in inconceivable pain the adopted son for whose guilt Jesus died. As on the day of the Incarnation, the love she had for her God became the love of Jesus, so on the day of the Redemption, the love of her Jesus became in her the love of the whole Church."

Thus it is that Mary is doubly a mother. She has given birth to Jesus, but she also has brought us forth to the divine. This conjoint maternity explains all. Mary is not the mother of a child for her-self, but of a child for us. She is mother of the Redemption before being the Mother of the Redeemer; rather, she is Mother of the Redeemer so that all the redeemed, united to their Head, compose only one Jesus. Speaking of the birth of the Savior at Bethlehem, St. Luke observes, "She brought forth her firstborn."[44] *First* implies

---

[43] St. Francis de Sales (1567-1622; Bishop of Geneva), *Treatise on the Love of God*, Bk. 5, ch. 4.

[44] Luke 2:7.

a second. The fecundity of Bethlehem called for the fecundity of the Annunciation and of Calvary; the maternity without pain called for the maternity in tears and in labor.

Listen! From His Cross, Jesus lets fall precious words! He has just broken the silence and speaks reverently to Mary.

Indicating to her the apostle John, He murmurs, "Woman, behold thy son!"[45] Oh, what strange words! Why, Lord Jesus, don't You say, "Behold someone who will act as your son, since I, as you see, am dying." No, You say, "Behold your son," as if to signify, "You lose me in my person, but you will find me again in the person of John."

Ah, John is not *only* John, but *each of us*, since, according to the doctrine of the Mystical Body of Christ, we must see in anyone in the state of grace not merely a simple human creature but Christ. "It is no longer I who live, but Christ who lives in me": *Non amplius vivit ipse, sed in ipso vivit Christus.*[46] Origen says in accordance with St. Paul, "The Christian is not simply a man, but he is another Christ." Jesus, John — we all constitute but one, only one Jesus and consequently for Mary, only one son.

The Savior, then, was right: *Woman, behold your son!*

"Jesus did not say," continues Origen, " 'Behold in the person of John *another son* different from me,' but simply, *your son,* as if He meant, 'You have only one Son, and I am He in this one. Through the mystery that I am going to accomplish, John is incorporated with me; he is in me, and I will live in him. You have, then, O Mother, in the person of John who is *at the foot of the Cross* the same Son who is *on the Cross,* your Jesus, whom you have brought forth and who is found in His disciples as the head is united to the

---

[45]John 19:26.
[46]Cf. Gal. 2:20.

members with which it is one. He lacks nothing to be identical with me, and since I am your Son, *he* is equally your son, and all those who will have the same title as John become from this moment, in me and with me, your only Son.' "

Is it possible to express more forcibly our life in Christ, our identification with the Savior, Jesus, in the unity of a single organism, of the same Mystical Body?

There is only *one* Jesus, the *whole* Jesus. The Mother of Jesus has only one Son, this great Jesus Christ the *whole*, of which the Savior is the Head and we are the members. Each member of Jesus has, then, in the most precise sense of the word, Mary for Mother.

To the words "Woman, behold your son," the other words are added: "Behold your Mother."[47]

---

[47]John 19:27.

Book II

The greatness of Mary's soul

God made Mary our Mother — and at what price we know. A mother is by nature one who gives. Mary is to be the great giver of the divine. To give, one must have; to share, one must possess. In view of the sublime role confided to Mary, dispenser of all graces, should not God endow her first of all with the most sublime supernatural riches? Should not divine life expand to the full in Mary before, through her, it expands in our hearts? *Esto concha, non tantum canalis.* "You must be a channel through which the divine gifts come to souls, be first the pastor, an inexhaustible well of the divine," St. Bernard advised Pope Eugenius III, who had been one of his monks.

Before considering Mary as the channel of supernatural graces, we must consider her as the personal receptacle of divine life. God made Mary what she is only so that she may give to others. Let us consider what she is, how God filled her with grace, and how she corresponded at every moment with her whole heart to all invitations to advance in grace.

Chapter Four

Mary's soul is free of sin

The point of departure for each of us in our advancement in grace is Baptism: baptism of water, the normal means; baptism of desire, its substitute. Every man comes into existence bearing the consequences of Original Sin, deprived by the sin of his first parents of the divine life God wished to give to man. Thus, born first to human life, he must be born again to divine life through the baptismal rite instituted to introduce man into Christian life, into the realm of the supernatural, into the family of the children of God.

Only one human being came into existence entirely pure: that is Mary. This incomparable privilege is called her Immaculate Conception. The Church does not wish to imply that Mary was conceived in the womb of her mother as she conceived Jesus Christ, through the operation of the Holy Spirit, for that would attribute to her a divine and miraculous origin like that of our Lord, and there is no question of that. The Church, in calling Mary immaculate in her conception, means that, from the moment Anna conceived her, she was preserved from any stain of Original Sin contracted by all the descendants of Adam and Eve. No one need be surprised at so beautiful a privilege.

Exclusive of the formal belief imposed by the Church, the reasons that militate in favor of the Immaculate Conception are evident. Did not Jesus owe it to His holiness to be born of a mother without stain? Would He, in whose sight even the angels are not pure, and who rejoiced only among the lilies, have consented to be born of one stained by sin? Who would believe it? Was not the Protestant convert right who said, "The mere supposition of a fault in Mary seems to me to reflect as an outrage on Christ, from whom she holds all her perfections and who did not blush to call her His mother"?[48]

Moreover, did not God owe it to His glory to preserve Mary from the blemish of Original Sin? What was the purpose of His coming to earth, if not to reduce to a minimum the empire of sin? Would His victory over sin have been complete if, even for a moment, the demon had been able to lay hold of Mary and deprive her of divine life?

Furthermore, did not Jesus owe it to His love for His Mother to preserve her from all stain of sin? In honoring her from all eternity, did He not do all in His power so that she might be absolutely pure?

Now she comes among us. "Take care, O Eternal Wisdom," cries Bossuet to the Word of God. "Take care lest even in this moment she may become infected with a horrible sin, that she may be in the possession of Satan. Prevent this evil through Your goodness; begin now to honor Your Mother; make it profitable to her to have a Son who is before her; because, in truth, she is already Your Mother, and You are already her Son."

Until the decision of December 8, 1854, the Church had left the firm belief in the Immaculate Conception to the free acceptance

---

[48]Miss A. Baker, *Vers la Maison de la Lumière*.

of the faithful, and although it was already authorized and had a special feast, it had not as yet been pronounced as a definite dogma.

From the early days of Christianity, until the tenth century, in fact, there are no explicit testimonials of Mary's privilege. In the Bible, the Mother of the Redeemer is promised as one predestined to crush the serpent's head, and it is readily agreed that her triumph over the demon would scarcely be effective if she herself had first been his victim. In the Gospel, the angel calls Mary "full of grace, blessed among all women."

Taken in the full sense of their meaning, these expressions logically include exemption from Original Sin; but all that the faithful concluded from the Bible and the Gospel was the marvelous holiness of Mary.

The exact idea of the immaculate preservation did not occur to them. Their attention was scarcely drawn to this side of the question; the problem had not yet presented itself.

It took the Middle Ages to bring full light from the controversies. Eminent theologians, such as St. Bernard and St. Thomas Aquinas, did not dare commit themselves and even inclined toward the negative, not believing that the privilege of Mary was evident from the texts of Scripture and the Fathers of the Church, nor that one might exclude the Blessed Virgin from the prediction of Original Sin, which is absolutely universal. The University of Paris definitely sided with the defenders of the Immaculate Conception, and in 1387, the university sent to the Pope, then at Avignon, several representatives, in particular Pierre d'Ailly and Gerson, to obtain the order that those who opposed the privilege of Mary might be denounced and prosecuted.

The first efforts to obtain recognition through the Church for the glorious title of Mary date from the Council of Bale in 1453. The Immaculate Conception was defined as a pious belief, in harmony with the cult of the Church, reason, and Holy Scripture, but the decree did not have the force of a law because of the schism into which the Council of Bale allowed itself to be drawn.

New steps were taken in the sixteenth century in the Council of Lateran, and at the time of the Council of Trent, Pope Leo X considered defining the dogma. They did not go that far, however, but merely declared in a negative way that they did not intend to apply the doctrine of the universality of Original Sin to the Blessed Virgin. A timid gesture, but an important one, which shows at least that the doctrine of the Immaculate Conception was not heretical or false, as several pretended it to be; but the pronouncement was not sufficient to impose it as a dogma of faith, nor even an incontestable belief.

The advocates of the privilege of Mary continued to come to the center of Christianity. Alexander VII published a bull deciding that the cult of the Immaculate Conception of Mary should be retained in the Roman Church, and he threatened with severe penalty those who opposed it. We later see such demonstrations of wholehearted approval as were given July 2, 1662, when the University of Douai, without hesitation, proclaimed thus through its rector the cherished belief: "Holy Mary, conceived without Original Sin, Mother of God and Virgin without stain, We, the Rector with the whole University of Douai, choose you today with one voice and one heart for our Queen, our Patron and Directress, and we are ready, in accordance with the exhortation of our Holy Father, Pope Alexander VII, and in concert with the greater part of the world, to profess and to defend always and everywhere your conception without stain."

Pope Benedict XIV drew up another bull, but it was reserved to the nineteenth century to see the hope of the preceding ages realized. Pope Pius IX named a commission to examine the question, and Rome asked the opinion of the bishops of the whole world. Of 626 answers, only four were negative, and these were later reduced to one.

On December 8, 1854, Pius IX in the presence of fifty-three cardinals and 143 bishops from all parts of the world solemnly promulgated the beloved dogma. Four years later, the apparitions to Bernadette[49] took place at Lourdes, and the Blessed Virgin confided to her in Pyrenean patois, the only language the little Bernadette Soubirous understood, *"Je suis l'Immaculée-Conception."*

We must guard against seeing in the incomparable privilege of Mary defined by Pius IX only a negative advantage, the absence of the sin of our first parents. The Immaculate Conception is a positive dignity of unequaled splendor for the Blessed Virgin. To say that Mary did not inherit the sorry privation of divine life, which had been the punishment of the Fall, is to say that she came into the world the recipient of supernatural life. The supernatural life that God gave her at the beginning of her existence was intensely rich in the divine.

From the very beginning, God the Father endowed her with all that would make her worthy to bear His only Son at the moment of His Incarnation. God the Son, eternally honoring her as His Mother, prepared her from the beginning for this holy and high dignity; and the Holy Spirit, looking upon her as His most perfect sanctuary after the holy humanity of the Savior, was pleased to enrich her with the maximum of His treasures. God gathered together all that had ever been granted and distributed among the

---

[49]St. Bernadette (1844-1879), Sister of Notre Dame who, in 1858, received eighteen apparitions of the Blessed Virgin Mary at Lourdes, France.

just souls and made a gift of it to the Virgin Mary at her entrance into the world.

"In this moment," writes Father Olier, founder of Saint-Sulpice and a great devotee of Mary, "God united and bestowed on her all the perfections He had given to all the just souls of the ancient law, so that she alone had more of the spirit of Christ than all the priests, patriarchs, judges, prophets, kings, all the saints of the Old Testament, and all the just of the Gentile nations ever possessed."

Down through the ages, God was pleased to enrich the different saints only so that, when Mary would appear, He might have greater joy in bestowing upon her all that He had apportioned to the just. To each of them the Most High had given some perfection. All these perfections He has gathered together, harmonizing them into a magnificent unity — the triumphal sheaf of Mary's graces.

"From the very moment of Mary's conception," says Father Olier again, "the Holy Spirit poured out on her more graces than all the most perfect and most eminent souls together ever possessed or ever will possess."

Such is the supernatural dignity of Mary from the first moment of her conception. Father Binet, an author who has written in a more lyrical strain[50] — rather excessively lyrical at times — warns the reader when he is about to speak of this prerogative of Mary: "Take care, because in speaking of her who was full of grace at her conception, we invariably fall into an abyss. Whether we speak of the quality or the quantity of the countless graces communicable only to the Mother of God, whether we try to explain the eminence or the almost infinite grandeur of each one of these graces, it seems to me that we will plunge into an ocean from whose

[50]*Chef-d'oeuvre de Dieu*, Pt. II, ch. 1.

depths we shall never emerge and so much the better; because we could not be more happily lost than in so sweet an ocean."

If the beginnings of grace in Mary were already incomprehensible, how shall we ever be able to evaluate her progress in grace?

Let us consider that every moment of Mary's conscious life was in full correspondence with God, that is to say that at each moment of her existence, each conscious breath intensified the divine presence that reigned in her with infinite splendor from the beginning.

What is sanctifying grace? It is a certain superelevation of our faculties to know and to love God; but more than that, it is the existence of a *something* — the presence of the great Someone, God Himself.

If the indwelling of the Holy Trinity in souls having the least degree of grace constitutes a marvel of marvels, what must we say of the divine habitation in Mary! Even at the moment of her conception, the divine life in her surpassed all that we could dream of and increased each moment of her existence. The Evangelist says of Jesus, "He grew in wisdom and in grace." How true that is of Mary, too!

Although all the saints achieved heroic heights in the supernatural life, yet none of them can compare to Mary in absolute correspondence with grace. St. Teresa,[51] so *faithfully* faithful in life and who died of love, could write the story of her infidelity to grace. One day, God presented St. Catherine of Siena[52] with a bunch of grapes, all of which were spotted, and He made her understand that it was a picture of her life — good without a doubt — but marred by imperfections that she could have avoided by more perfect cooperation with grace. The holy porter of the Jesuit College

[51]St. Teresa of Avila (1515-1582), Spanish Carmelite nun and mystic.

[52]St. Catherine of Siena (1347-1380), Dominican tertiary.

of Majorca, Brother Alphonse Rodriguez,[53] whom the Church canonized as a model of the love of God and of constant fidelity to the duty of his state, imposed upon himself the rule to kiss the stones of the wall of a certain corridor where he thought he had refused something to God or had not served Him wholeheartedly.

In Mary, there was no fault of any kind, no weed of infidelity in the harvest of her soul, nothing but perfect grains — complete failure for the sower of tare. The injunction "Be perfect as your heavenly Father is perfect" was never realized with more radiant or substantial fullness.

By reason of the role Mary was to have in the plan of Redemption, God not only enriched her supernaturally in a striking manner, but He gave her natural gifts that enabled her to develop and to enrich her magnificent divine life. Thus, Mary, endowed at the beginning of life with unparalleled sanctifying grace, was enriched at her entrance into the world with the full consciousness of her every act.

To cooperate with God and to perform meritorious acts, one must have reached the use of reason. Mary had the use of reason the very first moment of her existence, and that is why she could, although very young, place an act that of itself demanded full maturity of reason. This act which the Church commemorates on the feast of the Presentation of Mary, November 21, is the gift of herself to God in the form of a vow of virginity at the age of three or four years.

Who can measure the plenitude of this gift of her soul to the Most High! It is an official, exterior consecration to declare before the world the complete gift Mary made of herself to God every

---

[53]St. Alphonsus Rodriguez (d. 1617), Spanish wool merchant and Jesuit lay brother.

moment of the day, even while sleeping, thus verifying the words of the Canticle: "I sleep but my heart watcheth."[54] When the angel Gabriel asked her, eleven or twelve years later, if she were ready to *serve*, to give all, the swift answer came from her heart in words so sanctifying for herself, so glorious for God, so saving for us: *Ecce . . . Ancilla*. To serve? Behold, I am ready! She had been saying these words every moment of her life and constantly lived the reality hidden beneath them.

We might ask why God, who was to require motherhood of Mary, inspired her to consecrate herself to Him by the vow of virginity. It is not that marriage is wanting in holiness, because it is holy both in its divine institution as well as by its beautiful symbolism. The union of man with woman symbolizes, as St. Paul clearly explains, the divine espousals of Christ with His Church. Even though man has profaned this divine institution as he has abused other gifts of God, abuse does not condemn holy use. In Mary's case, would its use not have been most holy?

What, then, is the reason for Mary's vow of virginity? First, Jesus, having God for true Father, did not need another father according to the flesh. Secondly, it redounds to the glory of Mary to have the crown of her maternity enhanced by the sovereign and unique privilege of virginity. Moreover, the Fathers of the Church and the great theologians have always seen in the virginal and miraculous birth of Christ one of the fundamental reasons that her human nature was exempt from Original Sin, communicated only to men born of Adam according to ordinary generation. If, then, Christ had been born of the union of Joseph and Mary, He would not have been dispensed from Original Sin except by a special prerogative.

[54]Cf. Cant. 5:2.

If there had been no other reason for Mary's vow of virginity, would it not have been enough that God willed it so? How much greater is Mary because of her virginity! Never having shared her heart, Mary could give herself solely to God.

Chapter Five

Mary is full of grace

The perfection of Mary's correspondence to all the advances of God during her childhood and her youth can be understood, or at least surmised, from the little we have said.

What will be the elevation of the soul of the Blessed Virgin and the sublimity of her union with God in the future? We shall pause to measure it according to three memorable events: the Annunciation, the Nativity of Jesus, and the death on the Cross.

In considering the Annunciation, we need not review the exterior setting; a single detail will fix our attention: the angel Gabriel's salutation to Mary, "Hail, full of grace!" At her entrance into the world, Mary is filled with a plenitude of grace so great that we are lost in trying to conceive a proper idea of it, and we have seen that this plenitude increased at every conscious moment. At this time, however, Mary is to receive a new outpouring of the Holy Spirit.

St. Luke notes the angel's words in answer to Mary's question: "The Holy Spirit will descend upon you — *Spiritus Sanctus superveniet in te* — and the power of the Most High will overshadow you. Nothing is impossible with God."[55] What does this mean if not: "You are already filled to overflowing with divine grace, but now the Holy Trinity wishes to have a still greater place in you, wishes to unite Himself with your soul in a more royal manner. There is already plenitude; there is to be a new outpouring, a still more abundant fulness."

When we read the explanations of the Fathers and the Doctors of the Church on the profound mystery of the Annunciation, the most prodigious of the whole career of Mary, we notice that some seem to say that Mary already possessed *fullness of grace* when the angel appeared to her. Others say the salutation *gratia plena* meant that she was to receive this fullness through the descent of the Word of God into her womb.

The two opinions are true. Through the Incarnation and to qualify her for it, Mary was to receive, in virtue of her brave acceptance of God's plan, an unparalleled outpouring of the Holy Spirit. That does not mean, however, that before the divine message she was not already *gratia plena*. The Doctors of the Church do not base, merely on the message of the angel, their recognition of Mary's universal fullness of grace which she possessed and in which she increased daily from her Immaculate Conception.

The first Protestants, with Luther and Calvin, have tried to reject the interpretation consistently given by the Doctors of the Church to the words *full of grace*. Luther translates the word of the angel *Ave, Gratiosa* — "Hail, O thou beautiful one"; Calvin: *gratiam consecuta* — "Hail, O thou who hast obtained grace"; Theodore de Beze: *gratis dilecta* — "thou who has been gratuitously loved." These interpretations boldly deny the evidence and alter freely the meaning of the clearest expressions.

[55]Luke 1:35, 37.

The master of Don Scotus, the ardent William Ware of Warou, who was called *Doctor fundatissimus*, having treated the question of the Immaculate Conception with his students, said to them: "If I make a mistake in speaking of the Blessed Virgin, I prefer that it be in granting her too much, rather than too little, *volo deficere per super-abundantiam.*" The Protestant masters have preferred to minimize Mary's prerogatives. Let us leave them to their futile attempt.

At the message of the angel, Mary, always eager to correspond completely with the desires of God, opened her soul: "For an in-stant," writes Father Faber with becoming dignity, "Mary's blood was all her own. The immaculate young girl was not yet invested with the special prerogative of being at the same time virgin and mother. One awful moment sufficed to change all; from the pure blood of Mary the Holy Ghost formed the pure Body of Jesus; the human soul of Jesus sprang from nothingness . . . Until then, the Word had not condescended, if it may be so expressed, to become a part of His own creation."

At that moment, He accomplished the great plan He had formed from all eternity. Until that momentous hour, the Blessed Trinity had scarcely been revealed on the earth. God was uniquely the one God, *Deus unus.* The virgin motherhood of Mary, in mak-ing known the person of the Son, and in distinguishing Him for us from the Father, by all the personal difference peculiar to the invisible Divinity in heaven and the Divinity clothed in human-ity on earth, has made obvious the plurality of the Persons in God, their personal relation, and their substantial unity. Mary is the ostensorium of the Holy Trinity, not only because she held the Three Divine Persons as no other in the world, but because she has *manifested* the Three Divine Persons as no other.

If every motherhood is wonderful, what must we say of the motherhood in which Mary is the Mother, and the Son is God

Himself? Father Olier calls attention to the fact that some feasts are celebrated for one day only, others have an octave, and Easter is celebrated for forty days. To honor Jesus Christ hidden in the womb of Mary and adoring the eternal Father, the Church gives six months, for, from the Visitation until Christmas, she proposes for our adoration no other mystery of our Lord. The only exception to this is the feast of Christ the King, a very recent feast, celebrated the last Sunday of October. Could we say that six months is too long for the contemplation of so great a mystery as the Incarnation?

If Jesus, hidden in the womb of Mary, sanctified John the Baptist in the womb of Elizabeth, what must have been the sanctifying power communicated to His Mother, to whom He was bound by the most intimate union. Later, during the course of His public ministry, the sick touched the hem of His garment and at once they were cured, "and all the multitude sought to touch Him, for virtue went out of him and healed all."[56]

What wondrous sanctifying power was to emanate for Mary from the holy humanity of Jesus while this humanity was being formed in her womb! "Was it possible," notes a pious author, "that Mary could have conceived the Holy of Holies without having received a supereminent principle of holiness?"[57]

As the time for the humble and glorious Nativity approaches, the soul of Mary is increasingly enriched with divine treasures; she gives more to God each day, and each day God is pleased to give

[56] Luke 6:19.

[57] Abbé Gueric, Serm. IV in purif. V.M. — *Concepisse Sanctum sanctorum summa sanctificatio est.*

more to her. What sublime union with her Beloved Son as the poor family makes its way toward Bethlehem, the place of the family enrollment! What humble acceptance of the refusals at the inn! What perfect submission to the adorable designs of God, who willed that the Son of God be born about two hundred yards from the nearest home, in a roadside shelter for animals!

On this night of the Nativity, four oblations mount from her heart to God. The Virgin without stain offers herself to her Son; she knows that the Redemption will be accomplished through blood and the Cross. She offers her tears and her martyrdom for the salvation of the world in union with the sacrifice of her Son. Not content to offer herself to Jesus, she offers us with herself. She is conscious of her double maternity; she thinks of all her children: she is Mother of Jesus only to be our Mother — Mother of the *whole Jesus*. She unites all her children in a single maternal affection, so that there may be among them a single *fraternal* affection and, in her regard, a single *filial* affection.

Mary also offers Jesus to the Father — a unique form of worship! The Savior came to supply the homage that should have been offered by humanity and which humanity had refused to God. She takes possession of this oblation of the Head and invites all the members to offer themselves in common accord to Him, who is the Father of Jesus and our Father. Here, the altar is Mary's womb, and the Victim, Jesus: the Virgin in union with Jesus, the eternal Child and her Child, offering to God the One alone who can give to God glory worthy of Him.

One offering remains to her, one most dear to us: to present Jesus to humanity. All the living who will pass down the centuries are present to her, and to each one, she says, "Behold! the Lamb of God; behold Him who is born for you and who will die for you!" Thus, early she inaugurates her role of intercessor in Heaven and

Mediatrix between God and man, which marks *her supereminent place in the secret life of grace in our souls.*

If Mary's charity increased in a sublime degree during the nine months of *waiting,* what must be its ardor now that the Child-God is in her arms, and she can intensify one or all of her four oblations?

The splendor of Mary's sanctifying grace was blinding even at her Immaculate Conception . . . Since then, Mary has mounted higher and higher. To a plenitude, already full, succeeds an ever-increasing plenitude. "My chalice is overflowing," said a holy soul, "but I wish it held more." Mary's chalice overflows, but God always makes it capable of holding more.

It is impossible to consider all the events of the childhood of Jesus and the young motherhood of Mary: the Circumcision; the order to fly into Egypt; the flight to the distant country; the precarious home life in that country of false gods; the return to the village hospitality of Nazareth, where, in the future, the days will slip by uniformly, in so much the same way that one line in the Gospel will suffice to tell all: "The Child grew in wisdom, in age, and in grace." The Mother kept and pondered all these things in her heart, as the Gospel says in relating the principal episode of the hidden life: the loss of Jesus in the Temple and His teaching among the doctors.

"Son, why hast thou done so to us?"

And Jesus answered, "Did you not know that I must be about my Father's business?"

My Father's business, *Ea quae Patris.* What a wealth of reality is hidden in this expression! *Ea quae Patris.* The interests of the Father? Could not that mean the two beams of the Cross outlined against the sky twenty years hence? Surely the Boy-Christ would have used an evasive expression in order not to disturb Mary and

Joseph! The poor parents remained speechless: *Ipsi non intellexerunt verbum quod locutus est ad eos.* They understood not the words that He said. Mary will penetrate the awful meaning only little by little. One thing is obvious; today's separation is but the prelude to a more cruel separation: the departure for the public life and for all that will follow. *Ea quae Patris . . . Conferebat in corde suo. My Father's business.* How Mary will keep these words and ponder them in her heart! Her life is already one *Amen,* and the *Amen* will take on a still deeper significance.

When the day's work is done, the little family rests a while in the fresh air on the flat roof of the humble home of Nazareth, and occasionally Jesus takes up the *Torah* to answer the queries of Joseph and Mary. What maternal anguish wells up in the heart of the Virgin when He touches upon the sorrow of the Passion! Without doubt, Jesus avoids as much as possible this cruel subject, or, if He has to speak of it, He does so with infinite discretion. His efforts to conceal the frightening reality are futile. Under the most charitable words and the most filial consideration, Mary discovers the brutal truth; she sees the tragic reality. Since the prophecy of the sword of sorrows, she knows . . . or surmises. How indifferent words have a way sometimes of piercing the heart, of going deep into the soul! The Child permits it to be so to assist in the divine elevation of His Mother.

Years pass, peaceful, quiet years. Oh! relatively peaceful, we must admit, since they are menaced by vistas of pain lying beyond the hidden life. The Child will have to leave His Mother to begin his public life. What a heartrending separation accomplished with absolute submission to the divine will! The Cross is beginning to rear its grotesque form. But was not the Virgin created and put into the world for the Cross? Her *Ecce* increases in fervor. The only change discernible in Mary's soul is that it constantly becomes more deeply imbued with the divine.

When her hour comes, she stands with all her strength at the foot of the Cross. Our *stabat* is sung or read; hers alone is actually lived! During just three hours at the Foot of the Cross, how tremendously our poor divine Mother grows in love of God and charity for us.

At last, all is finished. Jesus has given up His soul. "It is consummated!"[58] The Savior has been taken down from the Cross. And Mary, seated on the corner of a rock, holds Him tenderly on her lap. This is the scene painters and sculptors call the *Mater Dolorosa*, the Mother of Sorrows. We must not be misled by the title, for the Mother of Sorrows must suffer less, now that Jesus is dead. The sorrow of the Child is the Mother's sorrow. Mary realizes that she is deprived of the human presence of Jesus, but *she* does not count. She thinks only of Him. He, her Child, has accomplished His mission. He cannot suffer any more. His whole life was a cross and the Cross has climaxed His life. From now on, the Cross, the agony, the death are passed. The Resurrection cannot delay. Jesus is already free from the throes of suffering — that alone matters. Joy is not yet Mary's portion, even though she has suffered so much. But if Mary does continue to suffer, Jesus does not suffer any more. Then can her *own* sorrow be called a sorrow? Jesus is happy forevermore. Mary is happy, too.

The *Sorrowful One* counts all the wounds and open sores on the lacerated body of the Savior: these marks of the scourge and those of the thorns, the spittle — repellant stains of blasphemous kisses, and even more hideous than the spittle — the kiss of Judas . . . All

[58]John 19:30.

these outrages and desecrations on the face and the body of Jesus, Mary gathers lovingly to heart. She has kept everything in her heart for so long; these, too, she will cherish. Ah! how consoled she is to have loved Him so much in order to expiate in advance all these terrible wounds of cruelty, of scorn, of forgetfulness, of betrayal.

The last consolation of holding Jesus in her arms must be denied her. The sepulcher is ready, and besides, evening is falling. Once again, Mary loses her Son. He is placed on the cold stone in the tomb of Joseph of Arimathea. The holy women are there ready to cover the lifeless body with a shroud. Before leaving the sepulcher, Mary lifts for a last time the brightly streaked cloth. Evening falls . . .

"Come, let us go, Mother!"

John, assisted by the holy women, gently supports *his* Mother. The guards roll the stone in place. The Virgin smiles wistfully through her tears in seeing the trusted guards of the Sanhedrin affix the seal that no one will violate.

Can the guards enclose, with a few tight bands and a little wax, Him who holds in His hands the whole universe? Guards, have confidence, no human hand will break the seal! God needs only God!

The gates of the city will soon be closed. They must go down quickly; it is the hour. Regretfully, Mary turns away.

Ah! She will often come back to the summit of Calvary. She will often retrace the steps of the morning's journey. Every day that she is in Jerusalem, she will make her pilgrimage to the place of the Crucifixion. We can see her as James Tissot, the artist, represents her, kneeling at the hole in which the Cross rested. There is nothing, nothing but the gaping earth . . . and this woman. Nothing but the abyss . . . and the Mother. Since the Friday of her sorrows, the heart of the Mother remained at the bottom of this abyss.

Imagine the void in the religion of Christ if there had been no *Mater Dolorosa* weeping for her dead Son, to teach the world how to mourn and to suffer. "A religion," says Monsignor Benson, "which would represent Mary with her living Child in her arms and would not give us Mary with the torn Body of her dead Son on her lap, would not be the religion to which we could turn when all else had failed." There are certain sufferings that one endures only because one has prayed for a long time near the Cross or at the site of the Cross.

The forty days that followed the Resurrection have slipped by . . . Jesus has ascended to Heaven. After the brief joys of the *glorious* apparitions, there is a new separation. Heaven has taken back its Word. The Mother of the Word must remain still longer on earth. Surely, the tender Mother must be brokenhearted at this separation. Mary finds in it another opportunity to offer herself and to sacrifice herself. Without a doubt, the joy of knowing her Son infinitely happy dominates all. Accustomed as she has been to live as *dolorosa*, she understands that she will cease to be the *Dolorosa* only when heaven will open to receive her, too.

There are still long days in perspective — long days of oblation, of merit, of sublime ascent in love.

Chapter Six

Mary grows in love through the sacraments

In the preceding chapter, while contemplating the progressive and continual elevation of Mary to God, we singled out three specific occasions on which, according to our judgment, the effusion of the Holy Spirit in the soul of Mary must have been most radiantly intense. Here again, because we cannot consider all the events of Mary's later life, we shall particularly note these three: the Descent of the Holy Spirit, the Holy Communions of the Blessed Virgin, and her Assumption.

We can distinguish in Mary a triple motherhood: her joyful motherhood at the crib, her sorrowful motherhood at the Annunciation and the Crucifixion, and her glorious motherhood in the Cenacle.[59] At Bethlehem, she gave birth to Jesus according to the flesh; at the Annunciation and Calvary, she gave birth to souls at

---

[59]The cenacle is the upper room in which the Holy Spirit descended upon Mary and the Apostles on the first Pentecost (Acts 2:1 ff).

the price of her crucifying acceptance; in the Upper Room, she witnessed the birth of the Church and guided its first steps.

The Holy Spirit communicated Himself to Mary for the first time in the home of her parents, Joachim and Anne, on the day of her Immaculate Conception. The second great effusion was in her humble dwelling at the Annunciation, when Mary uttered her *fiat* of immolation, which was brought to completion only on the hill of the infamous gibbet where her Son writhed in agony before the whole world. At Pentecost, again in prayerful seclusion, the Holy Spirit poured out upon her the infinite riches of His grace. May we not believe that, if her love for men hastened the first miracle of Jesus at Cana,[60] it is again her ardent desire that invites a swifter and more abundant coming of the Divine Consoler?

That is only a supposition, but one fact is certain: God willed to choose an identical abode for the spiritual presence of the Third Person of the Blessed Trinity and the sacramental presence of the Second Person. There are, as we know, two real presences: Jesus in the Sacred Host and the Holy Spirit in a soul in the state of grace.

This second presence, common to the Father and to the Son, is manifested visibly and more solemnly in the Upper Room than at Baptism, but is fundamentally identical in the baptismal infusion of the Divine Spirit in the soul made Christian. The presence of the baptismal fonts makes our churches most perfect images of the Upper Room. Formerly, the same Upper Room was the sanctuary of the eucharistic advent of the Savior and the descent of the Holy Spirit; now every parish church is a sanctuary of the sacramental coming of the Savior in the Host and of the spiritual coming of the Holy Spirit to the child being baptized.

[60]John 2:1 ff.

Mary grows in love through the sacraments

A tradition expressing theological truth, and one that adequately explains the painting by either Mignard or Lebrun and inspired by Father Olier, gives the following detail of Pentecost: Mary and the twelve Apostles are united in prayer at the cherished site of the institution of the Holy Eucharist. The Holy Spirit descends, and it is she, the queen, who receives first and entirely the outpouring from on high. A single tongue of fire above her forehead divides so that one part rests over the head of each of the Apostles. It is fitting to point out here all the glory implied thereby to Mary. The Holy Spirit comes to Mary, and God charges her, the Mother of the human family, with the distribution of all grace. What is true of the effusion of the Holy Spirit on that day is equally true of every outpouring of grace: God gives nothing to earth without first confiding it to Mary, without causing the gift to pass through her hands.

Is it possible to gauge the measure of the plenitude of the divine fullness in the soul of Mary on that first Pentecost? Less than ever before! The immense plenitude of grace in Mary's soul, unfathomable since her Immaculate Conception, has been increasing in a singular manner for fifteen years. It has been beyond measure since the superplenitude of the Annunciation — *Spiritus Sanctus superveniet* — a superplenitude that goes on increasing for thirty-three years, so that we might even say it approaches the infinite.

What can the Holy Spirit add to the divine life that is already hers? Nothing, according to our way of thinking, but in the eyes of God, Mary has not yet reached that degree of sanctity to which He wishes to raise her. That is why the Holy Spirit descends upon her again, and He who is abiding Love, the Love of the Father for the Son, expands the heart of Mary, increasing its capacity beyond human limits in order to enrich it immeasurably. It is not a question of enriching Mary's heart for herself, but of enriching it for us.

She has been the supernatural Mother of souls for thirty-three years, since the saving consent of the Annunciation, when the *Ecce Ancilla Domini* was heard for the first time. Her maternal function was only a power then; now she is going to exercise it on behalf of the present and the future needs of humanity down through the ages. With what generosity will she exercise it!

Words fail us in praising such immensity. They betray us, they forsake us, they seek refuge in a revealing and eloquent silence that prays . . . and in a prayer that is silent.

The effects of the coming of the Holy Spirit were more apparent in the Apostles than in Mary. They began to speak the various languages needed for those whom they were to convert. If the effects of the descent of the Holy Spirit were less conspicuous in Mary than in the Apostles, they were, nevertheless, more profound. The divine effusion made her pass, not as the Twelve, from imperfection to holiness, but from one sublime degree of perfection to another even more sublime and which, according to the words of St. Thomas of Aquinas,[61] *attingit fines divinitatis*, fringes on without quite attaining, of course, the limits of the divine life in God Himself.

Pure! Oh, certainly Mary was pure, the Virgin of the *Quomodo fiet istud*! How much more transparent is her purity now in the eyes of God. Humble! Oh, certainly she was humble, the gentle Virgin of the *exaltavit humiles*! But how much more humble now, after so many soul-stirring experiences and richer contacts with God have deepened her realization that all she is and has comes uniquely from Him who works within her. She abases herself in the knowledge of her own nothingness and of the infinite greatness of Him who is all-powerful.

[61]St. Thomas Aquinas (c. 1225-1274), Dominican philosopher and theologian.

Mary grows in love through the sacraments

Seat of Wisdom, Virgin most prudent, Mother most venerable: she has been all that for a long time. How much more now that the Spirit of wisdom, of prudence, and of holiness possesses her as an immense sea whose tides rise ever higher, whose conquering waves surge upward with constantly increasing powers.

The Virgin, since her consecration to God at the age of three, was filled with love for Him and souls, esteeming herself the servant of the Most High and of us all. But now who can conceive of her tremendous love for the Triune God, and for humanity, of whom she is the salvation, the consolation, and the refuge?

After Christ ascended to Heaven, Mary possessed Him only as all Christians possess Him — in the Eucharist. According to ancient tradition, Mary retired to the home of St. John or to the neighborhood of another apostle where she could, at each celebration of the *breaking of the bread,* participate in the renewal of the sacrifice and, by consuming the Victim, find again in Communion the ineffable joys of the intimate union of the nine months preceding the birth of Jesus.

The Incarnation was, in fact, the first union of the Virgin with the Living Bread *come down from heaven.* Not being a union through assimilation, it is not ordinarily referred to as Communion. Was not Mary the first chalice of the Blood of Jesus? Did not our Lord dwell in her during the nine months of expectation as in a veritable ciborium? How much richer was she than all the beautiful ciboria of gold or silver? At the Crib, was not Mary the first ostensorium of her Son, showing Him to the shepherds, to the Magi, and to the world?

Now she finds the past under another form; the consecrated Bread the Apostle places on her lips is Jesus formed from her own flesh and with whom her body is again united. The child is something of its mother, formed as it is from her own substance. In receiving the Body and Blood of Jesus, she finds again something of herself, and this *something of herself*, formed from her own substance, is the Body and Blood of the Man-God.

This Communion is absolutely unique in its kind and incomparably superior to any other union. We would try in vain to appreciate the benefit the Blessed Virgin received from each contact with her eucharistic Son. Ancient tradition mentions a special feast to celebrate the First Communion Day of the Blessed Virgin. History has recorded and tried to commemorate the value of the Communions of some saints, such as St. Stanislaus Kostka, St. Francis of Assisi, and St. Thérèse of the Child Jesus.[62] What is the ardent love of the saints compared with the devoted love of the Blessed Virgin at the sacrifice of the Mass or at Holy Communion? Catholic fervor will profit more by meditation on the beauty of the bond that unites Mary to Jesus than by the mere remembrance of Mary's eucharistic devotions in the mystery of the altar.

The Eucharist is a sacrifice and at the same time a sacrament. No one denies that, as a sacrifice, the Mass is identically the same oblation as that of Calvary: the Priest and the Victim are the same; only the setting is different. Jesus, the sole Mediator, willed to associate Mary with the Cross as the co-redemptrix; and, because God is faithful, this plan continues. Then, at every mystical renewal of the Sacrifice of the Cross — that is, at each Mass — the oblation of the Savior is made under the same conditions: Mary is present, keeping her station with Jesus.

[62]St. Stanislaus Kostka (1550-1568), model Jesuit who died during his novitiate; St. Francis of Assisi (1182-1226), founder of the Franciscan Order; St. Thérèse of Lisieux (1873-1897), Carmelite nun famous for her "Little Way" of spirituality.

Mary grows in love through the sacraments

As a sacrament, the Eucharist has for its object to communicate *life*. This life, our Lord, the God-Man, possessed because of the *fiat* of Mary, depending wholly on her free will. Again God is faithful, and His plan does not change. Each time Christ becomes present in the hands of the priest, the life given to us by the words of consecration comes originally from Mary. Is it not, then, through a special intervention of the divine Mediatrix, the Blessed Virgin Mary, that this life is communicated to us?

It would, therefore, be a fundamentally Catholic practice at Mass to offer Jesus to the Father through Mary: therein would lie the ascent of praise; and, likewise, in Holy Communion, to ask for grace through Mary: thereupon would follow the descent of favors and benedictions. We have Mary to offer, Mary to obtain; her intercession to raise to Heaven and her intercession to draw down to earth. At this moment and in the sacrament in which Jesus is most *Jesus*, would not Mary be active in the manner that would be most truly *Mary*?

Although each one of Mary's Communions was a heavenly joy, it was not yet Heaven. How could her body continue to contain a soul that so ardently desired union with the Eternal, face-to-face? It is impossible to explain, except as a sort of permanent miracle.

Why did God permit Mary to live so many years after the death and the Ascension of her divine Son? The first reason was probably that He willed through this long preparation for the Beatific Vision to increase immeasurably the Blessed Virgin's capacity for love. Having known the visible and continual presence of the Savior during thirty-three years, she longs with all her heart for the *great reunion*. The days pass; she must wait. As St. Augustine says, "God thirsts that we thirst for Him." May the Lord be praised, and may His thirst be quenched! The thirst of all the saints for Heaven in comparison with Mary's maternal and virginal thirst is as a drop of water lost in the immensity of the ocean, for Mary's yearning surpassed that of all creatures.

Bossuet gives us an idea of the intensity of Mary's consuming love in his magnificent sermon on the Assumption, in which he explains how love which gives life also causes death. In this connection, the mystics describe the torments of a soul that has come close to God, were it only a single instant, and felt in His radiance such a need for the invincibly attractive. All that thereafter the soul is consumed by a yearning desire, a torturing thirst.

Earth is the land of outstretched arms for every human being, and it is this which makes for the hope as well as the joy and the torment of existence here below. What must it be for one who, better than anyone else, has understood true values to whom henceforth nothing is as nothing and *all things else* are *over and above*. The Kingdom is seen in the true light.

While thinking of the suffering of ardent souls, a suffering that attained terrific intensity in Mary, Bossuet turned to God and could not but cry out, "Ah! How cruel You are!" No, it is not cruelty, Mary will live on love, a constantly increasing love that, although it is her very life, causes her to die at every moment. A perpetual miracle is required so that her soul does not separate from her body under the force of the love that threatens to crush her physical frame and to give flight to her soul. And Mary will continue to be ravished by love until the last moment, when, no longer able to love on earth, she will find Heaven at last.

There is another reason God left the Blessed Virgin on earth for a number of years after the Ascension of the Savior. He wished that she preside over the initial development of the newborn Church.

Huysmans aptly says:

The Blessed Virgin accepted the weighty task that Jesus bequeathed to her, namely, that of mothering the child born upon the Cross, the Church. She received it and for twenty-four years, according to Saint Epiphanius, or twelve years according to other saints, like a loving grandmother, watched over this frail little being that the *New Herod*, the Universe, sought from all sides to strangle. She formed the Church, she planned its trade of fisherman of souls; she was the first mariner of the little boat which was beginning to launch out on the great sea of the world. When she died, she had been both Martha and Mary. She had united the active life and the contemplative life, and that is why the Gospel of the Mass for the feast of the Assumption is justly taken from the passage of Saint Luke in which he tells of Christ's visit in the home of the two sisters. Her mission was then complete. The Church, in the hands of Saint Peter, was sufficiently developed to sail without towing.

Not that Mary was the chief bishop of the Church. No, not at all. Peter was the head of the Church; Mary was a motherly counselor, but her protection was not less divinely precious because of its unofficial character.

Death came at last to the Blessed Virgin. There are no authentic details of the circumstances surrounding the sleeping away of the Blessed Virgin other than the tradition reported by St. John Damascene[63] and introduced by the Church into the Office of the Breviary for the fourth day of the octave. The Apostles had

[63]St. John Damascene (676-749), Greek theologian, orator, and philosopher.

dispersed to the different parts of the world and, at the death of the Blessed Virgin, were transported in a moment to Jerusalem, where they assisted at the funeral of their queen. Thomas, who was not with them, arrived three days later and begged to see the Mother of Christ in her tomb. All the Apostles went to the sepulcher of our Lady and rolled back the stone that covered the tomb. What consternation! The body of the Blessed Virgin was not there. Nothing was left but the marks of the blessed remains, the shroud, and a delicious perfume; the body had been miraculously taken to Heaven.

Is it not strange that God permitted the Blessed Virgin to be subject to death? Would it not have been more glorious for her and for her Son if she had ascended to Heaven without undergoing the separation of body and soul, a consequence of Original Sin? Immaculate — dispensed from the stain of Original Sin and its consequences — how could she become the prey of death!

Since Jesus died, it was fitting that the Mother imitate her Son in that, as in everything else, and be treated like Him. That is the first and principal reason. Another reason is, without doubt, that God wished to give us as a model for our death and as a support in our last moments, not only the death of Jesus, but also Mary's death. Is it not a great comfort to know that Jesus and Mary have gone before us by this door through which we all must pass?

Can we still question why the body of Mary was not subject to the usual corruption of the tomb? Mary was immaculate. Was it becoming that the body of the Virgin, the receptacle of a pure soul be the prey of worms? Moreover, had not this body been, through the splendor of the sanctifying grace that was Mary's, the most beautiful ciborium of the Triune God? Was it not, through the miraculous intervention of the Holy Spirit in the Incarnation, the marvelous reliquary that bore the Child-God for nine months?

We generally believe that Mary was carried to Heaven by angels. Why carried to Heaven? Would it not have been better if she had ascended herself, by the strength of her perfect nature? It was proper that there be a difference between Jesus and Mary, and that the Assumption be distinguished from the Ascension.

Now that we have followed the Virgin Mary to Heaven, it remains to us to contemplate her there and to study her in her maternal mediation.

Book III

Mary's motherly heart

A mother's heart! What a glorious marvel of grace is the heart of a mother. Poets of every language have tried to extol its grandeur.

In the first act of *d'Angelo*, Victor Hugo eulogizes a mother's love in this exuberant outburst of appreciation:

> However worthless I may be, I had a mother. Do you know what it is to have a mother? Did you have one? Do you know what it is to be a child, a poor, weak child, naked, forlorn, hungry, alone in the world, and to feel that you have near you, around you, bending over you, walking when you walk, stopping when you stop, smiling when you cry, a woman . . . no, you do not realize yet that it is an angel who looks at you, who teaches you to speak, to read, and to love, who warms your fingers in her hands, your body on her lap, your soul in her heart! Who gives you her milk when you are little, her bread when you are big, her life always! To whom you say, "Mother!" and who says, "My child!" in a tone so gentle and sweet that God Himself rejoices over these two words.

Chapter Seven

Mary comforts us

An English author tells the story of a mother who tried the incredible in order to save the remains of her child: "The boy had been hung for robbery and buried outside the Christian cemetery. The mother went to look for his remains. Upon being rebuked for her action, she exclaimed, 'The flesh of my flesh had disappeared, but the bones of my bones remained. I stole them from the custody of the authorities. Tell me, do you call that a theft? My little boy, the bones of him whom I nursed, the bones of him whom I saw smile and cry. They belong to the authorities? No, they are mine, not theirs! They have lived in my womb!' Then she told that, as her son was being led to execution, he cried out, 'Mother! Mother!' This cry had been ringing in her ears constantly since his execution. Now that she had buried her son in consecrated ground, she had more confidence in the goodness of God. She had suffered so long, but the Lord knew all about it."

This Polish legend, too, is very significant: "A young boy called several doctors for his mother, who had lapsed into a coma. One doctor prescribed a particular treatment, but the other doctors said it would be better to let her die than to subject her to such a treatment. A second doctor suggested another remedy to which the others made the same objection. Then the son, in utter distress, screamed, 'Mother!' At her son's voice, the mother awoke and was cured."

These are striking examples of the power of a son over his mother, and the untiring labor of a mother for her son — a labor that nothing can daunt or diminish, not even the blackest ingratitude of the most ungrateful children.

If the heart of any mother is an abyss of indulgence and goodness, what must the heart of Mary be? Mary's influence is sovereign in the realm of mercy. God owes it to Himself to be *just* as well as *merciful,* but Mary is not obliged to temper her mercy with justice. When a soul is in distress, Mary intervenes. We need not be endowed with special merits to obtain her intercession; the more destitute we are, the more indulgent she is; the less we deserve her help, the more merciful she proves herself.

Mary is frequently pictured with her head inclined toward the earth, and her hands filled with graces. At Valencia in Spain, the people venerate a statue of the Blessed Virgin under the title of *Notre Dame de los Desemparados.* They call their Madonna the *gobba,* or the hunchbacked, because the Virgin is so accustomed to stoop to us mortals.[64]

Upon the door of the lower Sainte Chapelle at Paris, there is also a statue of the Virgin inclining her head toward earth. A pious tradition relates that a little girl wanted to place a wreath of flowers on the head of the Blessed Virgin. Mary bent her head to

---

[64]The condemned are permitted to say their last prayer before her, and one day, while one of these unfortunates was kneeling at her feet, just before his execution, the Blessed Virgin struck five times with her lily against the crystal globe covering her; and the outcast, an innocent man, was recognized as such.

receive the crown and remained fixed in this attitude, which, no doubt, she liked.

In its own way, another little legend tells how granite can serve the mercy of Mary! A sculptor, working on the scaffolding of a cathedral, suddenly leaned too far back, lost his balance, and fell; happily, a statue of the Blessed Virgin, with arms extended, caught the falling man.

It is a popular belief that Mary can refuse nothing. The poet Charles Péguy walked to Chartres to obtain from the ancient Madonna there the cure of his son, and the favor was granted. He might have imitated the good woman of the *Golden Legend* who prayed Mary to free her son, a prisoner. The boy did not come back at once, but the good woman did not give up. She took the little Bambino from the arms of Mary: "My son has been taken away from me, and you have not brought him back! I am taking your Son, and I shall keep Him as a hostage." The story goes on to say that, naturally, the Madonna went at once to get the prisoner and to bring him back to his mother.

What an enormous anthology of all the cures and temporal graces obtained through Mary could be compiled! At the Parisian sanctuary of Our Lady of Victory, a confraternity was established in 1837, and in 1886, there were already fourteen thousand ex-votos of marble. Is not Lourdes a peerless proof of the power of Mary? Although it is impossible to mention even a few of these stories of Mary's power, we shall not omit this little story related by the Count de Champfeu, a captain of the frigate, who got it from the Admiral Dorlodot des Essarts, then a young ensign of a ship in the naval division of the Pacific and a witness of the episode.

It happened when sailboats were in the last stages of their use. A rigger in the crew of one of these sailboats fell from the topmast into the water. The rest of the crew, who were on their way to their hammocks at the time, rushed to his rescue. Although they had on deck only two life buoys, having lost the others near Cape Horn, they threw both of them into the sea. By clinging to one of them, the man was saved. That was fine, but where was the second life buoy? They looked for it all night. Finally, at dawn, they spotted the life buoy bobbing along on the water, and, to their consternation, midshipman Jacques de Langelle, completely exhausted but still clinging to it miraculously. After resting awhile, he solved the mystery. At the cry, "A man in the sea," he had jumped from the chain-wale of the mizzen to rescue him. The crew was too much interested in their efforts to save the rigger to notice him. Langelle thought that, after the rescue of the sailor, the whaleboat would be directed in search of the other life buoy. Imagine his dismay when he saw the frigate set up sail, pull in the gangplank, and turn in an opposite direction. He screamed wildly, but distances are great at sea; darkness fell rapidly, as it does in the cold countries where there is no evening.

Langelle thought himself alone and lost forever. His despair increased when he realized that his absence would not be noticed, since there was to be no evening service. The crew would think he was sleeping in his hammock on the deck. He grew sick with fear and, in his fatigue, was tempted to let himself go. This deep, clear water attracted him; the stars seemed to dance on its surface. One of his hands had already relaxed its feeble hold when Langelle thought of his mother. He raised his eyes to the stars, whose gentle light comforted him and prayed to his heavenly Mother, his Mother among the stars, *Stella Maris*. Strengthened by faith and confidence in the Blessed Virgin, he managed to struggle in the chill water until morning. When the stars dimmed their light, the frigate was beside him. The morning star, *Stella Matutina*, had saved her faithful servant.

If the Blessed Virgin shows herself so maternally loving in bestowing temporal graces, how much more loving and attentive
must she be in giving supernatural help!

Art has always taken delight in representing the mercy of
Mary. Sometimes the scene is charming in its simplicity, as is the
painting at the museum of Montefalco, near Foligno, in which
Mary, armed with a club, is forcing a big, black, horned devil with
hooked hands and feet to release a child whom he threatens with
his lance, as the child endeavors to reach Mary for refuge. On the
other side of the demon, a woman — the child's mother, no doubt
— with hands joined in an attitude of prayer, implores Mary's
help. Similar to this is the picture of Castel Ritaldi dating from
1509 in which the mother weeps and begs for mercy while the
devil forces a hook into the little limb of the child.

In depicting the Blessed Virgin as Divine Protectress, artists
sometimes present Mary surrounded by small groups of especially
privileged souls: the benefactors or friends of the artist, or members of a confraternity; in other pictures, a whole nation claims
Mary's protection. The better to accentuate the maternal vigi-
lance of the gentle Virgin, some artists represent Mary protecting
sinners in the folds of her cloak. Sometimes the mantle is supported by angels, while powerful protectors lead the trusting people to the feet of the Madonna, and God's wrathful arrows break
on the Virgin's cloak. How truly is she Our Lady of Perpetual
Help!

Mary is also a most powerful intercessor. Above the famous
door of Rheims, Mary is represented as kneeling in the attitude of
supplication, pleading with our Lord on the day of the Last Judgment. Behind her, an angel carries the Cross in both hands to

remind the Savior of the co-redemptive agonies of His Mother during the sorrowful days of the Passion.

Real facts, however, are more impressive than all these symbolic representations. We shall mention only one. With his usual charm in storytelling, Father Doncoeur relates that, after his ambulance had been captured at the battle of Guise in 1914, a German Major pointed out to him in a nearby field an abandoned wounded French soldier whose head was black with blood, the upper part of the face having been badly shattered. Father knelt down: "My son, it is I, the chaplain of the 115th."

"Ah, it is you! All night long in the pouring rain, I said my beads that you would come!"

The wounded soldier died a few minutes later, repeating, "I am happy."

These examples of outward assistance impress us, but what must we think of the interior graces granted without any exterior evidence: help in temptation, support in difficulties, various lights for the progress of the soul, strength to counteract the influence of the demon. Mary never fails to help.

An old picture, dating from 1610, represents Mary seated with her Son at her side. Mary has her foot on the head of the serpent, and Jesus has His foot on His Mother's, as if to show the harmony of their double effort. The same significant detail is found in the masterpiece of the artist Erasmes Quellin, in the church of St. Michael at Louvain.

If we look for a simple explanation of the singular efficacy of the intercession of Mary in our behalf, it can be found in two words: *power* and *goodness*. She can do everything for us and wishes to do everything she can. Without goodness, power would be worth nothing; without power, goodness would be weak. Mary possesses these two qualities in a supereminent degree.

"How could she but be powerful," St. Bonaventure cries out, "she who merits the triple title: Daughter of God, Mother of God, Spouse of God?"

Daughter of God. When the Most High looked for one to whom He might entrust His Word, He thought of Mary. Having given her this Treasure, what lesser treasure could He refuse her? Since this divine Treasure is the Redeemer, how could the Father refuse the graces of the Redemption to Mary? What would be the purpose of sending a Savior to earth, if not to grant the salvation of mankind? Could it be possible that Mary's request for the salvation of a redeemed soul would not be heard?

Mary is not only the daughter of God but also the *Mother of the Son.* She can say to the Word Incarnate what the Father alone could say to the Word: *My Son.* The words of the psalm that only the Most High could utter in the heights of Heaven, Mary can repeat since the first Christmas night in the stable of Bethlehem, not with the same meaning, but with just as much truth: "Thou art my Son. This day have I begotten thee."[65] Could such a Son refuse anything to His Mother? Has He not promised to hear anyone who asks for the grace of salvation? Scripture recommends to every man not to forget the groanings of his mother.[66] If that is true for every man, would it not be doubly true for the Son of Man?

Omnipotent intercessor with the Father and the Son, Mary is likewise omnipotent in her intercession with the Holy Spirit, for is she not His *spouse*? When, at the Annunciation, Mary placed her vow of virginity in opposition to the promises of maternity, the

[65]Ps. 2:7: *Filius meus es tu, Ego hodie genui te.*

[66]*Gemitus matris tuae ne obliviscaris* (Eccles. 7:29).

angel calmed her with the assurance that the Incarnation would take place through the divine intervention of the Spirit of love and infinite holiness. From that moment, Mary became the Immaculate Spouse of love personified — the Sanctifying Spirit. Now she intercedes for her earthly children: *Veni, Sancte Spiritus*. "Descend, Holy Spirit; see this soul in distress."

Does not Holy Scripture say, "The prayer of a just man availeth much"?[67] Then with how much more reason the prayer of the Immaculate Spouse!

What would power avail without goodness? What would be the use of Mary's queenly sway over the Most High if her love for us did not incline her to use it in perpetual intercession?

Mary is our *Mother*. To some, this means merely that Mary feels toward us as any mother feels toward her child. They look upon this idea as a pretty figure but nothing more, not a fact to be taken literally. Such an opinion is far from the truth. Mary is in all reality our Mother.

What is a mother? One who gives life. Is it true that Mary has given us life? Yes, certainly; not natural life, of course, but supernatural life — the life of the Holy Trinity in our souls, which consists in grace on earth and glory in Heaven.

At a given moment in the history of the world, it depended on Mary, solely on her, on the free consent of her will, whether or not grace would be granted to us through Jesus Christ. By this consent of Mary we were born to divine life. She *is* in the strictest sense *our true Mother*.

Becoming thus our true Mother at the price of labor and tears, Mary received from God, in harmony with her title, the sentiments her role demanded. We can picture our most amiable

---

[67]Jas. 5:16.

Mother perpetually occupied in heaven with the salvation of her poor children on earth. From on high, she looks down upon these *little ones* to whom she gave birth in her greatest sorrow . . . One of her unfortunate children is in mortal sin. The end of his life is approaching; his hour comes. Oh! if death were to strike him in mortal sin! Then Mary hurries to God. "Look, my Lord, to save this unfortunate child, I have given all the tears of my heart and all the Blood of my Son! That is a great deal! If this poor child is lost, my tears, the Blood of my Son and Yours are lost forever! Oh, no! Have mercy on me! Have mercy on us!" How could God resist such a supplication?

One day, a grief-stricken mother from Thecua threw herself at the feet of King David: "O King, save me."

"And the king said to her: 'What is the matter with thee?' She answered, 'Alas, I am a widow-woman, for my husband is dead. And thy handmaid had two sons: and they quarreled with each other in the field, and there was none to part them: and the one struck the other and slew him.

" 'And behold the whole kindred, rising against thy handmaid, saith, "Deliver him that hath slain his brother, that we may kill him for the life of his brother, whom he slew, and that we may destroy the heir"; and they seek to quench my spark which is left . . .' "

Mary speaks in a similar strain: "Lord, I had a Firstborn. His brothers have killed Him. Jesus died on Calvary and, if my other children are lost, whom shall I have left?"

Holy Scripture, speaking of David, adds, "He answered the Mother from Thecua, 'As true as Jehovah is living, not a single hair of your son will fall to earth.' "[68]

Would Jehovah be less merciful than the servant of Jehovah?

[68] 2 Kings 14:4-7, 11 (RSV = 2 Sam. 14:4-7, 11).

Chapter Eight

Mary intercedes for us

There is no doubt that Mary was associated with Jesus in the acquisition of redemptive grace. That is not all, however; she is equally associated with our Lord in the distribution of grace.

In the cycle of Original Sin, the sin was committed by Eve, consummated by Adam, and transmitted through Eve. In the supernatural order, the cycle is identical. Redemption is begun by Mary, consummated by Jesus, and transmitted through Mary.

It does not follow, however, that the acquisition of grace and its distribution are necessarily inseparable. God might have willed that Mary give us Jesus and that Jesus remain absolute Master of the graces acquired at the price of His own Blood. Such was not God's plan. Bossuet sums up the tradition when he says, "God willed to give us Jesus Christ through the Blessed Virgin Mary, and since God is faithful in His gifts, this order does not change. It is and always will be true that, having received the universal principle of grace, through her charity, we now receive, through her mediation, its various applications in all the different states of Christian life. Having, in her maternal charity, contributed to our salvation through the mystery of the Incarnation, which is the universal principle of grace, Mary will contribute eternally in all other operations of grace which are necessarily dependent upon the one."

Speaking with full authority, Pope Leo XIII in his Encyclical of October 1891 says, "By reason of her consent to divine Motherhood, we may with equal justice assert that out of the great treasury of all graces, which the Lord has brought to us through this Mystery, nothing whatever is bestowed upon us except through Mary."

But if the importance of Mary's intervention is so great, is not the role of our Lord diminished?

The Catholic Faith formally declares, according to St. Paul, that there is one Mediator, Jesus Christ. To give foundation to its refusal to adhere to the Marian credo of the Catholics, the Protestant Reform argues that, by placing a mediatrix on a par with Christ and attributing to her the same efficacy of action, the Mediator is no longer unique and too much is accorded our Lady. The Protestant Reform seriously misunderstands the doctrine. In the first place, although Mediatrix, the Blessed Virgin was nonetheless redeemed herself. She exercises great power in obtaining the salvation of souls, but first she herself needed to be redeemed.

St. Paul is right: *There is one Savior, one Redeemer.* Mary has benefitted as well as all have by the Redemption. She is different only in this: her redemption has been *more sublime*, as Pope Pius IX says in the Bull that defines the Immaculate Conception. It consisted in preserving her from every stain of sin from the very beginning of her existence.

Being redeemed in the passive sense, as we all are, does not prevent Mary from becoming redemptrix in the active sense. To question Mary's active role in the Redemption evidences a gross lack of understanding, since every baptized person, whoever he may be, has his share of responsibility in the salvation of the world. Each one of us, by the very fact that we are one with the Savior, cannot but be a savior with Him: a secondary savior, of course, but really and efficaciously a savior. This does not take away anything from the merits of Christ. Moreover, without detracting from His power, it makes His mercy marvelously resplendent.

His own power is not diminished in any way; His own merits are merits of *strict justice*: they alone have efficacy capable of furnishing an adequate and complete compensation for the injury done to God by sin. Our Lord is willing, nevertheless, to call upon our collaboration under the triple form of exterior zeal, prayer, and sacrifice. The merits of these acts are not saving in strict justice; they are so only by divine complacence, because our Lord wills to consider the multiple contributions of each one of His members and to use them for the salvation of souls.

It follows, then, that if every Christian owes it to himself — if he would fully understand his vocation as a Christian — to be a *redeemer* with Christ, why should anyone be surprised that Mary, the creature blessed among all women and so closely united to our Lord, is called upon to participate in the Redemption like us, only more splendidly and more efficaciously? No one likes the word *co-redemptrix*; it seems to indicate equal collaboration. That may be, but we may disregard the word itself — the reality alone is important. Nothing is easier to admit than the mediation of Mary in the salvation of the world, since God asks the least of us to be mediators.

The mediation of Mary, however, rises to sublimity, with all the splendor of her unique role. St. Bernadine of Siena[69] says, "From

---

[69]St. Bernadine of Siena (1380-1444), Franciscan friar whose powerful preaching helped reform fifteenth-century society.

the moment she conceived the Word of God in her womb, she obtained a certain jurisdiction, a sort of authority over every temporal possession of the Holy Spirit, to such an extent that we receive the grace of God only through Mary."

Our need for Mary, our Mother and Mediatrix, is expressed simply by the child to whom the Sign of the Cross was being taught: "In the name of the Father, and of the Son, and of the Holy Spirit . . . Mamma, there is no Mother!" There is a Mother. She is not mentioned in the Sign of the Cross, but she exists and the Catholic Church gives her a special place of preference.

Failure to recognize Mary is one of the great weaknesses of Protestantism. It does not admit that she is Mother and Mediatrix of the members of Christ. A sad religion, this religion that has no mother! Many Protestants, no doubt, share the sentiments expressed by the great Newman in the following incident. While Newman was a tutor at Oxford, before his conversion, his brother Francis came to live with him, while continuing his studies. Newman placed a large picture of the Blessed Virgin in the student's room. In answer to the complaints of his young brother, Newman inveighed against Protestants who were forgetting the words: "Thou art blessed among all women!"[70]

Jesus alone merited, in the strictest sense of the word, the restoration of our supernatural life. That is a fact which cannot be overlooked in defining the power of Mary.

What places the Blessed Virgin uniquely above all the elect, on a plane so elevated that it is beyond human appreciation, is that God asked her free consent to the Incarnation and the redemptive plan. That is the reason for the superiority of Mary's mediation over that of the saints.

---

[70]Thureau-Dangin, *Renaissance religieuse en Angleterre au XIXe siècle*, 25.

Likewise, the mediation of Jesus is superior to the mediation of Mary. The difference does not lie in the extent of the mediation; the mediation of Jesus and Mary is equally universal. In other words, every blessing, every salutary grace comes to us through Mary as well as through Jesus. The essential difference lies in the intrinsic quality and efficacious value of Marian mediation. Christ's redemptive activity was complete; that is, its satisfaction was one of *perfect equivalence* because of His *condign merit*, whereas Mary's redemptive activity was more purely supplication, effective because of her *equitable merit*, or what we might term her rights of friendship.

Thus, the merits of Jesus make demands of the Father; the merits of His Mother present petitions. Jesus demands, Mary asks. Christ merited our redemption, then, in *strict justice;* Mary, through *pure impetration.*

The true place of Mary in Christian dogma was revealed to the converted soldier, Ignatius of Loyola, while he was preparing in the solitude of Manresa to become the great saint we know him to be. He gives the following account of his prayer:

During the night, I felt myself drawn by a strong sentiment of great confidence in our Lady. The next morning, before, during, and after Mass, I experienced great devotion and tears. A vision of our Lady and her Son, ready to intercede with the Father, was granted me. It seemed to me that the two Mediators invoked the Father for me, and I have good reason to believe that I saw them. My soul was seized by a great devotion for the Mediators, the Son of the Father and His Mother. While I prayed the Mother with her Son to intercede for me with the Father and then prayed the Son with His Mother to intercede for me, I felt myself carried to the Father . . . I saw and felt that our Lady was propitious to me in her intercession with the eternal Father. During the prayers of the Mass addressed both to the Father and to the Son and at the moment of the Consecration, I could not but feel and understand that Mary is the source and channel of grace.

If Mary is so powerful, how is it possible that souls are lost? If she is "Mother of God to obtain all, Mother of Man to give all," would not salvation be certain for every soul? No, God Himself even consents to be checked at times by the human will.[71] Mary, who intercedes and entreats, is not more powerful than God. When Mary pleads with the Heart of God, she is sure to be heard, but, in pleading with the heart of man, she is often repulsed by an obstinate will.

In trying to explain this problem, the great Portuguese orator Vieyra cried out, "What a blessing for the good thief and what an eternal loss for the bad thief that our Lady stood between the cross of the good thief and the cross of Christ. Christ was between both thieves, but when the Mother of God was between the sinner and God, then only was the sinner saved; when she was not there, the sinner was lost."

The thought is beautiful but merely symbolic. The text must not be taken too literally, lest we believe that there are sinners for whom Mary does not pray; that the Blessed Virgin, foreseeing in the light of God a certain man's obstinacy in his sin, would refuse to intercede for him, thus conforming herself to the eternal decree. Even then the Blessed Virgin would intervene. She gives up

---

[71]This is only a temporary and very obvious opposition. God will have the last word! "Penance or punishment."

only in the last extremity when truly, if ever this happens, there is nothing more to do.

The extent of Mary's intervention is, then, practically limitless; the efficacy of her mediation is similarly without bounds, although there are certain conditions attached to its operation which her clients would do well to consider. Protestants and Jansenists, as, for example, Pascal in the ninth letter of his *Provinciales*, and Nicole in his notes to the Latin translation of Pascal, accuse Catholics of pretending that a few exterior signs of devotion to Mary are enough to assure eternal salvation. Some authors and preachers, we must admit, expose themselves to this criticism. They do not affirm that these exterior practices are enough in themselves, but they let it be understood that Mary infallibly obtains final perseverance for those who observe them. Some distinction, however, must be made.

A true and constant devotion to Mary is a moral indication of predilection,[72] since *true* devotion supposes horror for sin and *constant* devotion supposes a horror for sin until death. Although this is not peculiar to Marian devotion, since every true and constant devotion implies this fidelity, nevertheless, devotion to Mary contains a particular virtue to preserve solid piety and stainless purity.

Let us suppose someone is living in sin and has not the courage to quit his miserable condition, but he clings faithfully to the practice of praying an *Ave* every month. Since he recites it with faith, it is a real prayer. Will his prayer be heard? St. Alphonsus Liguori, an authority on devotion to Mary, thinks this sinner's loss morally impossible.

[72]See the Sermon on the Scapular by St. Claude de la Colombière. We say *morally*, because the Council of Trent (sess. 6 — ch. 12, can. 16) observes that a revelation is necessary for absolute certitude that one will persevere in grace.

A charming story told in the life of the Curé of Ars seems to verify this opinion. One day, a lady in deep mourning was waiting in church when the saintly Curé, vested in surplice, leaned over her and said, "He is saved."

The lady was troubled. "He is saved, you say?" A gesture of unbelief was her only comment.

Then, carefully articulating each word, the Curé repeated, "I tell you he is saved. He is in Purgatory; we must pray for him. Between the bridge of the parapet and the water, he had time to make an act of contrition. The Blessed Virgin obtained this grace for your husband because, even though he was irreligious, he sometimes joined in your prayer at the May altar erected in your room. That merited for him contrition and final pardon."

Very different is the situation of the habitual sinner who would say, "I can live as I please and do what I want, since an *Ave* will save me." Never has Catholic belief attached any moral assurance of salvation to such formalism based on presumption.

That is what St. Alphonsus explicitly states: "When we declare that it is impossible for a servant of Mary to be lost, we do not mean those who, by their devotion to Mary, think themselves warranted to sin freely. We say that these reckless people, because of their presumption, deserve to be treated with rigor and not with kindness. We speak here of the servants of Mary who, to the fidelity with which they honor and invoke her, join the desire to amend their lives. I hold it morally impossible that these be lost."

Nicole asks, "What shall we say of the maxim that if one wears a particular habit in honor of Mary, one will certainly be saved?" He answers himself, "We must say that it is a serious error." Why? His reason is simple enough: "Because it is wrong to say there is an eighth sacrament in the Church."

Nicole was referring to the scapular. We know that in 1251, at Cambridge, the Blessed Virgin appeared to Simon Stock, the Superior General of the Carmelites and, in giving him the scapular, said to him, "He who dies wearing this habit will be preserved from eternal perdition." Seventy years later, Pope John XXII judged the affirmation worthy of faith, and more than twenty sovereign Pontiffs supported his pronouncement.

What must we think of such a privilege? Some interpret the text literally: "He who dies wearing this habit will not be lost . . ." For Father Claude de la Colombière, there is no restriction: "One may lose one's scapular, but one who wears it at the hour of death is saved."

The common interpretation follows the opinion of Pope Benedict XIV. The text does not mean: "One who limits himself to that," but, "This practice, harmonized with the duties of one's state of life, will become a source of salvation." It is clear that he would have no right to salvation who would confine himself presumptuously to the promise made to St. Simon Stock, and would give himself up to sin, and refuse the last rites of the Church on his deathbed. A hundred scapulars would not save the impenitent sinner from eternal perdition. But the question is precisely whether the wearer of the scapular would ever come to this state of final impenitence. This prayer of St. Alphonsus to Mary gives the true note:

> I know if I always invoke you,
> you will come to my aid,
> and you will make me triumph.
> But I fear most that I may not think
> to invoke you in temptation.
> The grace, then, that I ask of you

and dare demand of you,
most Holy Virgin,
is that I think of you always,
and particularly in my combat with Hell.
Grant that, in the midst of the combat,
I may call upon you continually
and say without ceasing,
"O Mary, help me!
O Mary, come to my assistance!"

No sinner who wears the scapular will die impenitent, but a sinner who is determined upon impenitence will surely die without the symbolic habit of the servants of Mary.[73]

The Rosary also has singular power, although not the same type of guarantee of efficacy. War had been waged against the Albigensians for sixteen years, but it was impossible to conquer them. While St. Dominic[74] in 1202 prayed in the Chapel of Notre Dame de Prouille, he heard a voice: "Go, preach my Rosary, and you will be more victorious than Montfort and his crusades." Dominic obeyed. The Albigensians began to retreat and were conquered.

Before the time of St. Dominic, chains of beads were used for prayer. The founder of the Friar Preachers added meditation on the mysteries, and for a century and a half, the devotion spread everywhere. After 1350, however, it fell into disuse. It was the Dominican André de la Roche in Brittany and the Venerable John

---

[73]Since 1910, the cloth scapular may be replaced by a medal properly blessed for this purpose and bearing an image of the Sacred Heart of Jesus on one side and of the Blessed Virgin on the other.

[74]St. Dominic (c. 1170-1221), founder of the Dominican Order, or Friars Preachers.

Sprenger, the Prior of Cologne on the Rhine, who, in the middle of the fifteenth century, restored the splendor of the Rosary, which was never lost again.

With the Litany of Loreto and other shorter prayers as, for example: "O my Queen, my Mother" of Father Zucchi or the *Memorare* of a religious of Clairvaux, perhaps St. Bernard himself, the Rosary is the most popular devotion to the Blessed Virgin Mary. Father John Svenson, the author of the delightful *Récits Islandais*, affirms, "In Denmark, a Protestant country, where I have been a missionary for twenty years, a great number procure these chaplets and recite them every day. It is an actual fact that if these persons remain faithful to this devotion, all without exception are converted and come into the true Church. One of two things happen: either they give up the practice of saying the Rosary, or they become Catholics."

Even if some Christians are too complacently satisfied with exterior practices of religion almost entirely devoid of spirit, a formalism rightfully attacked by Christian adversaries and wrongly confused with true Catholicism, true Christians know, without disregarding the practice, that devotion to Mary, like every other authentic devotion, is one of spirit and life. Our Lord wants adorers "in spirit and in truth."[75] Practices are necessary because we are not all spirit, we are partly body; but precisely because we are body, we too easily materialize all that we touch; we must exercise constant effort to maintain spiritual perspective in our devotions. Let us beware of mechanical routine and force ourselves to spiritualize and to animate, in the deepest sense of the word, each one of our practices of devotion.

[75]John 4:23.

Chapter Nine

Mary obtains grace for us

Now that Mary dwells in glory, does she obtain for us only such graces as pertain directly to salvation, or does she intervene to obtain every grace?

There is no doubt that Mary's influence extends to every grace. By the very fact that she is the Mother of God, she is the Mother of the Author of grace and, consequently, the Mother of all grace without exception.

Strictly speaking, can we say that *all* grace comes to us through Mary? Unhesitatingly we answer *yes*.

A very fundamental reason underlies this belief: a reason, at once simple and sublime, whose profound beauty does not astonish us, now that we are enlightened on the doctrine of the Mystical Body of Christ.

Two facts are certain: Mary is a mother. She is the Mother of the *whole Christ*. That is basic, for from this proposition, we can deduce the twofold truth: that Mary has something to do with all the graces that come to us and that nothing comes to us *except through Mary*.

The explanation is simple: Christ cannot be divided.

She whose mission it is to *form Christ* cannot isolate the Head from the members, nor form the *Head* and forget the *members*. It was Mary's role to give birth to Christ and to care for Him. That was her duty toward her *Firstborn*; it is likewise her duty toward us, her *second-born*.

Ask any mother if the work of training and caring for a child is not one of constant details. If the mother knows her duty — and who would know it more splendidly and accomplish it with more love and delicacy than Mary — does she leave to chance the least of these details? Does she omit, under pretense of being interested in more important phases of the child's development, the thousand little attentions that reveal more than anything else the true mother?

It is Mary's maternal mission to nurture every baptized soul which she has brought forth to divine life so that Christ is formed and increases in him. Mary cannot, therefore, refrain from intervening to secure those graces which will make each soul more Christlike.

How can Mary's two maternities be separated? It is inconceivable that Mary would have left nothing undone to help Jesus become most completely *Jesus* and would concern herself little to make us more like to Jesus. Mary gives the same attention to her *second-born* that she gave to her *Firstborn*. The sphere of application is different, but the love is the same. Mary is not like us; she does not distinguish between the Head and the members of Christ. The sword of Solomon is unknown to her. She is too much a mother for that.

If a pagan could say, "Nothing concerning man is foreign to me," how much more truly is Mary interested in all that concerns us. Nothing concerning mankind is foreign to her. Nothing that takes place on this poor earth escapes her. She is acquainted with our life in this valley of tears. Her life among us only increased her desire to come to our assistance by every possible means.

We do not think it unusual that St. Thérèse of the Child Jesus should say, "I wish to spend my Heaven in doing good upon earth. I will let fall a shower of roses upon the earth." No one hesitates to admit that she has done what she promised, she who is so gentle and sweet, so powerful over the Heart of God.

And Mary? If such is the role of a humble little virgin, what may we expect from the Queen of Virgins? It would be very unreasonable to imagine that Mary is limited in her action to certain graces only. It would not be like Mary to say, "These roses I shall scatter; the others I shall keep in my hand. They would be too much for my children."

There are, besides, Scripture texts to support this theological reasoning. *Et erat Mater Jesu ibi:* "The Mother of Jesus was there" — she was with Jesus. The Magi and other contemporaries of Jesus fully realized this. Even before the birth of Christ, while Mary still bore Him in her womb, she obtained the sanctification of John the Baptist. The Mother of God was there; she is everywhere. Mary is at the first miracle; she is at the foot of the Cross; she is in the Cenacle. Mary's presence at every vital occasion in Christ's life gives us to understand that her influence must be felt everywhere. Since this truth is so evident, it seems useless to insist upon further proof.[76]

---

[76]In virtue of this principle, St. Ignatius does not hesitate in his *Exercises* to give a meditation on An Apparition to Our Lady soon after the Resurrection. It is not mentioned in Scripture, but Scripture supposes that we have intelligence. *Scriptura supponit nos habere intellectum.* Suarez says, *"Ubi res ipsae et opera quibus Christus matrem honoravit clamabant, verba non erant necessaria":* Why should one express in words what facts make evident?

Tradition interprets and develops with singular completeness the implications of the Scriptural proof for Mary's power. It focuses attention upon a precious detail of the promise of a Savior which God gave to man soon after the Fall: the prophetic promise speaks more about the Mother of the Redeemer than about the Redeemer Himself. "I will put enmities between thee and the woman, and thy seed and her seed; she shall crush thy head."[77]

Because of these words, many Fathers of the Church bestow upon Mary the title New Eve. The text proves equally the role of Mary as collaborator with the Mediator at the hour of Redemption. Although it does not prove her universal mediation, it does point to her maternal function in the divine plan of Redemption.

As to the nature of this maternal function, two possibilities suggest themselves. It might be thought that once the Savior entered into His role, Mary would disappear and no longer actively concern herself about mankind. She would be Mediatrix for a time, but her role would cease at her entrance into Heaven, where she could look on but do nothing. Again, it might be thought that, when the Savior began His work, Mary would continue hers. She worked with Him on earth; she would continue to work with Him in heaven. It is in accordance with the divine plan that she help to distribute what she helped to acquire.

Mother of the Redeemer, Mary is also and more truly Mother of the Redemption. Why imagine that her connection with mankind is severed when she enters Heaven? Could there have been so much for her to do when she was on earth and nothing to do now that she is in Heaven?

Oh, no! She is Mother of the Savior and fulfills her part wherever Jesus is Savior. *Mater Jesu ibi.* Wherever Jesus saves, the Mother is

[77]Gen. 3:15.

there to assist with her maternal mediation. The plan of God is *one*; God is faithful to Himself.

In referring to this beautiful privilege of Mary, the saints and the Doctors of the Church give her a rather unusual title: *Mystic Neck of the Church*. In the natural body, life flows through the neck to the other parts of the body, and by means of it, the parts of the body are connected with the head. It is a channel for respiration and the means by which nourishment reaches the exhausted bodily forces. It receives, further, certain honors not given to the rest of the body. The child clings to the mother's neck when troubled by fear or drawn by love. All this may be applied perfectly to the Blessed Virgin. Thus, Corneille de la Pierre explains it in agreement with St. Jerome, St. Bernard, St. Albert the Great, St. Bellarmine,[78] St. Bernardine of Siena, and St. Liguori.

The comparison, however, is not exact in one respect. The neck, as the natural connection between the head and the other members, operates without its own will and intelligence. Mary is an intelligent and willing bond between our souls and Christ.

Much could be gleaned from the abundant harvest of tradition to supplement the explanations of the Doctors and the Fathers of the Church, of whom we shall quote only a few. For the Eastern Church, we have the words of St. Germain of Constantinople: "No one is saved, no one escapes danger except through you, O Mother of God; no gift is obtained from Heaven except through you, O beloved Mother of the Savior."

For the Western Church, we have these well-known texts: St. Bernard: "It is the will of God that we receive all through Mary";

[78]St. Jerome (c. 342-420), Doctor who translated the Bible into Latin; St. Albert the Great (c. 1200-1280), medieval theologian, philosopher, and scientist; St. Robert Bellarmine (1542-1621), Jesuit Cardinal, teacher, and writer.

St. Peter Damian[79]: "No grace comes from Heaven to earth without passing through the hands of Mary"; St. Ambrose[80]: "Through her, all graces come to earth"; finally, St. Bonaventure: "All that comes to us from Heaven comes through Mary."

Prayer is another proof for this dogma, for as we believe, so do we pray: *lex orandi, lex credendi.*

It was a great joy for the clients of Mary when Pope Pius IX defined the dogma of the Immaculate Conception of the Blessed Virgin on December 8, 1854. Some wondered what new jewel the subsequent ages could add to the crown of Mary, their Mother. This new jewel was added when, in 1921, the Pope approved the feast of Mary, Universal Mediatrix of all divine grace. At the Marian Congress in 1904, and then again in 1913, some reports had been presented to this effect. Soon after, under the initiative of the Primate of Belgium, Cardinal Mercier, a petition was addressed to the Holy Father, Benedict XV, asking him "to pronounce in Catholic dogma the traditional belief of the Christian people in the universal intercessory Mediation of Mary with the unique Mediator of justice, Jesus Christ."

A Mass proper to this feast was authorized for May 31 and accorded first to the churches of Belgium and then to all churches of Christendom. Pope Benedict XV inscribed the feast on his own calendar and appointed a commission "to prepare, to promote, and to obtain the solemn definition."

Pope Pius X, the illustrious predecessor of Benedict XV, affirmed, "Mary is the heavenly channel through which all graces descend to earth."

---

[79]St. Peter Damian (1007-1072), abbot and Cardinal-bishop of Ostia.

[80]St. Ambrose (c. 340-397), Bishop of Milan.

In bringing together all these affirmations and in comparing the abundance of these texts with the dearth of ancient proofs in favor of the Immaculate Conception, a learned theologian was surprised "that the Immaculate Conception was able to progress while her mediatorship of graces had not yet been established as a dogma of faith." The sweeping assertion, "All grace comes to us through Mary," seems beyond question. Mary can rightfully be represented as Sister Catherine Labouré saw her in 1830 in the chapel of the Daughters of Charity, rue du Bac, Paris. Here is preserved in a beautiful painting the memory of Sister Catherine Labouré's vision of the Blessed Virgin as dispenser of grace. Her dress is white, her mantle the color of dawn; the serpent is crushed beneath her foot; her arms are outstretched toward the earth, and a beautiful brilliant light radiates from her hands covered with rings of costly jewels. "Behold," Mary had said to Catherine, "the symbol of the graces that I shed upon those who ask for them."[81]

"All grace comes to man through three perfectly ordered degrees: God communicates the grace of Christ; from Christ it passes to the Blessed Virgin; from the hands of Mary it comes to us."[82] The recent work of the sculptor Debert, for the Chapel of the *Orantes de l'Ave Maria* at Bry-sur-Marne, expresses perfectly this beautiful idea of the dogma: at the top is God the Father, of whom we can see only the face and the extended arms; below, the Holy Spirit in the form of a dove with wings spread; then Jesus with His hands nailed to the Cross. The Blessed Virgin stands on the world, her head reaching as high as the Heart of her Son, catching in her

---

[81] There were also on Mary's hands some diamonds that had no light or sparkle: "They represent," testified Catherine Labouré, "the graces man forgets to ask of her."

[82] St. Bernardine of Siena.

cupped hands the precious graces which, through the Father and the Holy Spirit, descend from the wounds of Jesus in the form of drops of blood to be scattered by Mary in a rain of redeeming grace.

Several questions arise concerning this all-inclusive fact of the universal mediation of the Blessed Virgin. It is perfectly clear that all the graces we ask through Mary's intercession come through her. But what of the graces we ask without calling on Mary in particular — for example, those that we petition through some other saint? Even then Mary intervenes. Benedict XV solemnly pronounced this doctrine. The Sacred Congregation of Rites hesitated for two years to attribute to Jeanne d'Arc[83] one of two miracles proposed for the process of her canonization because one of them had taken place at Lourdes. On April 6, 1919, the Sovereign Pontiff, after reading the decree authenticating the miracles, expressed himself in this way:

> If it is fitting to recognize in all special favors the Mediation of the Blessed Virgin through whom, according to the Divine Will, every grace and every benefit comes to us, we cannot deny that in one of the miracles mentioned, the Mediation of the Blessed Virgin is manifested in a very special way. We think the Lord permitted it to remind us that we must never exclude the memory of Mary even when the miracle seems to be attributed to the intercession of one of the Blessed or of a Saint. Even when God is pleased to glorify one of His saints, we must suppose the intervention of her whom the Holy Fathers have called the Mediatrix of Mediators, *Mediatrix mediatorum omnium*.

---

[83]St. Joan of Arc (1412-1431), French heroine who led the French army against English invaders and was burned to death for alleged heresy, but later declared innocent.

What of the graces we obtain without asking? It is Mary again who obtains them for us. Her mediation, although different in its efficacious value, as we have noted, possesses the same universality as the mediation of Jesus. All graces come through Jesus; all graces come through Mary. The Blessed Virgin is perpetually busy *on the edge of Heaven* sending us graces.

Only when earth will be no more will the Blessed Virgin rest. With his sweet smile, the saintly Curé d'Ars, reflecting a profound theology, said, "I think the Blessed Virgin will rest at the end of the world, but as long as there is an earth, she is being pulled at from all sides. The Blessed Virgin is like a mother with many children; she is continually going from one to the other." He naively admitted that he himself had gone so often to this source that there would be nothing left if she were not inexhaustible.

One detail confuses many. Is Mary's part in obtaining grace *necessarily actual?* Father Terrien, one of the theologians who have spoken best and most profoundly on the subject, in his imposing work *Marie, Mère de Dieu, Mère des Hommes*, distinguishes between cooperation in grace and actual cooperation in every grace in which he treats of the mediation of Mary considered as "an exercise of her maternal duties."

Not one grace comes to us unless the Blessed Virgin has her maternal part in it. Is this part necessarily actual? Father Terrien dares not say so definitely, while others state plainly that this point deserves definition as a dogma. To speak otherwise would be to admit a limitation in our Lady's exercise of her maternal function, which nothing authorizes.

An interesting historical detail supplements this discussion: On December 13, 1920, Cardinal Mercier presented the Pope with a plan for the Office in honor of Mary Mediatrix. Pope Benedict XV studied it carefully and, on the seventeenth of January, said to the cardinal in receiving him, "I have read your whole plan; it is beautiful. There is no reason to hesitate; it must be approved." Then he added almost timidly, "The Invitatory[84] is the only part I do not like so well. That is only a personal impression; you need not consider it."

Since the cardinal insisted upon hearing the Pope's criticism, the Holy Father continued, "Well, this is it: the most beautiful and most classic invitatories almost always reproduce the *Venite Adoremus* of the psalm. I regret that you have not observed this, because I would like to see the adoration of the Son associated with the mediation of the Mother."

That same evening, Cardinal Mercier modified the Invitatory to read: *Christum Redemptorem qui nos omnia voluit habere per Mariam, Venite adoremus!* "Come, all ye faithful, to adore Christ the Redeemer who wills that we come to Him through Mary!"

---

[84]The Invitatory is a sort of refrain repeated at each stanza of the hymn that opens the matins in the breviary.

Conclusion

The love of Christians for Mary

One of the most devoted apostles of the Blessed Virgin, the blessed Louis de Montfort, did not hesitate to say, "God wishes that Mary be at present more known, more loved, more honored than she has ever been. If our Lord is not known as He ought to be, it is because Mary is still unknown. It is she who brought the Savior into the world the first time; a second time, in the modern age, she will give her Son to the world . . ."

The Blessed Virgin has been venerated in all ages. Her cult began in the devotion of Jesus for Mary.

With what love the Apostles and the first faithful surrounded the Divine Mother! Pious tradition has it that the Basilica of Our Lady of the Pillar was built under the inspiration of St. James; at Tripoli, St. Peter himself is supposed to have consecrated a church in Mary's honor which is still existing. There is at Arles the debris of an old temple known under the name of Our Lady of Grace (or of St. Honorat of the Alyscamps) which formerly bore this inscription: *Hoc sacellum dedicatum fuit Dei parae adhuc viventi* — "This chapel was dedicated to the Mother of God in her lifetime."

In reality, the official devotion to Mary was not regulated until rather late. Not before the sixteenth century do we find the establishment of feasts with a very definite character, such as the Nativity, the Purification, the Annunciation, and the Assumption. But there is nothing astonishing in that. Until the end of the fourth century, the martyrs only were honored in public devotions. As soon as the Church began to honor the non-martyr saints, Mary was given a place of honor in the cycle of the Liturgy.

Mary's most glorious titles spring from Christian hearts. These titles nearly always recall the Madonna's power of intercession: Help of Christians, Mother of Divine Grace, Refuge of Sinners, Source of Life, Gate of Heaven.

Christian fervor in a transport of enthusiasm for Mary varies indefinitely its happy findings; title follows upon title; and for no other reason than to let their imaginations, or rather their hearts, speak, the faithful, that is, the entire laity, has welcomed before its formal definition the dogma of the universal mediation of their Queen. What "theology" in the titles: Our Lady of Grace; Our Lady of All Grace; Our Lady of Perpetual Help; Our Lady of Good Counsel; Our Lady of Peace; Our Lady, Help of Christians; Our Lady of Consolation; and a thousand other appellations of the same nature.

Within the city of Constantinople alone have been discovered the remains of at least fifty-eight sanctuaries that had been dedicated to Mary; in the environs of the city, about twenty were found bearing such cherished names as Our Lady Full of Grace; Our Lady of Prompt Success; Our Lady of Good Hope; Our Lady, Living Earth; Our Lady, Source of the Infinite; Our Lady of Pity (*Eléousa*); Our Lady, Liberator of Sorrows; Our Lady of Bounty; Our Lady Merciful.

In France, aside from the centers that attract the crowds, there exist no fewer than thirteen hundred churches and chapels in honor of Mary. What shall we think of these magnificent cathedrals — these litanies of stone? We can say of nearly all of them what Vauban said of the Cathedral of Saint Mary at Coutance: "Who is the sublime fool that threw that marvel into the air?" As soon as one temple is finished, another is built. Sometimes these churches dedicated to Notre Dame rise out of the earth simultaneously and mount toward Heaven as a single yet multiple outburst of praise.

Michelet could define the Middle Ages as "an act of faith in the Virgin translated into stone."

The Medieval cathedrals do not represent the work of particular persons, but rather the radiant unanimity of Christian people who wished to build these splendid monuments to our Lady. "The poor gives his arm, the rich his money, the clerk his knowledge, the artist his genius. There is nothing like it in the history of art."[85]

In a page that rises like a steeple, Ozanam,[86] visiting the country of the Cid, celebrated this glory of the cathedrals which sing Mary's praise:

> O Notre Dame of Burgos! You are also Notre Dame of Pisa, and of Milan, Notre Dame of Cologne, and of Paris, of Amiens, and of Chartres, Queen of all the large Catholic cities; yes, truly, you are beautiful and gracious *Pulchra es et decora*, since the mere thought of you has made grace and beauty descend into the works of men. As barbarians, these men came out of their forests and, burners of cities that they were, they seemed made only to destroy. You have made

[85]E. Male.

[86]Bl. Frederic Ozanam (1813-1853), French scholar and founder of the Society of St. Vincent de Paul.

them so gentle that they have bent their head beneath the stones; they have yoked themselves to heavily loaded carts; they have obeyed masters in order to build your churches. You have made them so patient that they have taken no heed of the centuries in order to hew beautiful portals, galleries, and spires for you. You have made them so bold that the height of their basilicas leave far behind the most ambitious edifices of the Romans and at the same time so chaste that these great architectural creations, with their statuary people, breathe only purity and immaterial love. You have disarmed a great number who found glory only in spilling blood; instead of a sword, you have given them a trowel and a shears, and for three hundred years, you have kept them in your peaceful workshops. O Notre Dame, how well God has rewarded the humility of His handmaiden! In return for the poor house of Nazareth where you lodged your Son, what rich dwellings has He given you!

For the most part, "the masters of the work" remain unknown. It is better so, for thus the entire Christian people, in a mingled and touching anonymity, offered an enduring prayer wrought in stone, a prayer that stands erect as Mary stood, and that nothing, neither the squalls of inclement weather nor the squalls of bombs, has succeeded in bringing to earth.

From the temples of stone, we must penetrate into the sanctuary of souls. In each Christian heart, there is an altar erected to Mary. Enter a Catholic church, and look at those who are praying. If fifty persons are present, twenty-five will have a rosary in hand; and half of the remaining number, you may be sure, are likewise invoking the Blessed Virgin. For a goodly number of the faithful, to pray means *to pray to Mary.* And indeed who would reproach them for it? Is it not Dante, the theologian poet, who wrote "To hope for a grace and not to address oneself to Mary is to wish that the desire should fly without wings"?

Sometime before his holy death, St. Francis of Assisi had an ecstasy. He saw two ladders, similar to those of Jacob, which touched the earth at one end and the sky at the other. Above the one, our Lord appeared; above the other, His most holy Mother. A number of friars minor were endeavoring to mount to Heaven by the ladder at which our Lord was seen; but after having climbed several rungs — some more, some less — all, overcome by the glory and the majesty of the God of virtues, could not advance and were obliged to descend. Upon seeing this, the saint exhorted his children to have recourse to Mary, the Mother of God. For his part, St. Francis Xavier,[87] apostle and patron of the Propagation of the Faith, proclaimed that there is no conversion possible without Mary. "I have found," he writes, "that the people rebel at the Gospel every time that I forget to show the image of Christ's Mother next to the cross of the Savior."

Anyone so imprudent as to seek to persuade the faithful that Mary occupies too much place in their piety would have little chance of being understood. Besides, what are their regrettable omissions of tribute compared with the cries of love, of veneration, of tender respect, of filial confidence, of dazzled admiration, that rise from noble souls? If Catholicism possessed only this marvel — Mary — would it not tower from a height without limits, over every other religion?

---

[87]St. Francis Xavier (1506-1552), Jesuit missionary to the East Indies.

A Jewish-convert writer, killed in 1916, gives apt expression to this thought:

> Catholicism alone has made a place in its devotion for the Virgin and, by so doing, it has replaced maternal love in the feminine heart and the figure of a woman at the peak of the ideal temple. Woman, under her double ideal, virginity and motherhood, has begun to rule over men, exercising upon their hearts a profoundly appeasing influence. Humanity hastens around a robe ... Who can deny the new sweetness that this cult has brought to men? Woman softened the hearts of knights, and to her influence we can trace all the refinement of our race. Yet, what is woman in comparison with her who is the *Gate of Heaven*, the *Star of the Sea*, the *Morning Star*.[88]

Art under all forms tries to glorify Mary. There is no school of sculpture or of painting that does not possess its multiple Madonnas. Raphael, who died at thirty-eight, found time to paint more than thirty pictures of the Blessed Virgin. We must confess that he sometimes found his inspiration in unworthy types for a subject so pure; often, however, we find in him real evidences of piety. For example, he asked to be buried at St. Mary of the Martyrs in the shade of the statue of Notre Dame.

This Marian piety of Sanzio is not at all an isolated case. Every mystery, every attitude, every expression of Mary has challenged the interpretative powers of countless artists. Someone reproached Michelangelo for giving Mary too young an air in his *Pietà*. "You forget," he answered, "that virginal and immaculate, Mary was not blighted in the least by sin; an air of perpetual youth is the only

[88]Marc Boasson, *Lettres de Guerre*.

thing that befits her." It is indeed true that under multiple and multiform representations, Mary is for us the most perfect picture of the eternal youth of God.

Louis de Montfort believed that the end of the world was near, since renewal of devotion to Mary would be the preparation for the conversions necessary before the last cataclysms. We are more inclined to believe that the world is only at its beginning. The Gospel is just beginning to shine. Everything is to be done. It is therefore not an end that is foreshadowed, but an aurora which is rising. The world wants more evangelical substance and, in those places where the Gospel has already penetrated, a better evangelical life.

In this conquest, who will aid most efficaciously, both in extent and in depth? Mary.

⊰⊱

Raoul Plus
(1882-1958)

Raoul Plus was born in Boulogne-sur-Mer, France, where he attended the Jesuit college. In 1899, he entered the Jesuit novitiate in Amiens and was ordained there. Because of laws that persecuted religious orders at that time, Fr. Plus had to leave France in 1901 and did not return from this exile for ten years, during which time he studied literature, philosophy, and theology in Belgium and Holland. He also taught courses in the field of humanities.

During World War I, Fr. Plus enlisted as a soldier, and subsequently as chaplain, and was awarded the Croix de Guerre and the Medaille Militaire for his heroism. After the war, Fr. Plus taught religion at the Catholic Institute of Arts and Sciences in Lille and became a well-loved spiritual director for the students.

Fr. Plus wrote more than forty books aimed at helping Catholics understand God's loving relationship with the soul. His words consistently stress the vital role of prayer in the spiritual life and seek to show how to live out important spiritual truths. His direct, practical style renders his works invaluable for those seeking to know Christ better and to develop a closer union with Him.

An Invitation

Reader, the book that you hold in your hands was published by Sophia Institute Press.

Sophia Institute seeks to restore man's knowledge of eternal truth, including man's knowledge of his own nature, his relation to other persons, and his relation to God.

Our press fulfills this mission by offering translations, reprints, and new publications. We offer scholarly as well as popular publications; there are works of fiction along with books that draw from all the arts and sciences of our civilization. These books afford readers a rich source of the enduring wisdom of mankind.

Sophia Institute Press is the publishing arm of the Thomas More College of Liberal Arts and Holy Spirit College. Both colleges are dedicated to providing university-level education in the Western tradition under the guiding light of Catholic teaching.

If you know a young person who might be interested in the ideas found in this book, share it. If you know a young person seeking a college that takes seriously the adventure of learning and the quest for truth, bring our institutions to his attention.

www.SophiaInstitute.com
www.ThomasMoreCollege.edu
www.HolySpiritCollege.org

SOPHIA INSTITUTE PRESS

THE PUBLISHING DIVISION OF

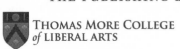